DIGITAL

D ISRUPTION

IMPACT ON BUSINESS MODELS, REGULATION & FINANCIAL CRIME

DIGITAL

D ISRUPTION

IMPACT ON BUSINESS MODELS, REGULATION & FINANCIAL CRIME

....EDITED BY

DAVID CHAIKIN & DERWENT COSHOTT

AUSTRALIAN SCHOLARLY

Contents

Preface

It is generally accepted that scholarly debate on digital disruption can be traced to Professor Clayton Christensen in his 1997 book entitled *The Innovator's Dilemma: When New Technologies Cause Great Firms to Fail.* Professor Christensen's ideas concerning the effects of disruptive technologies on existing and future markets have permeated into government policy making, boardroom discussions and popular discourse. The revolutionary impact of technology has been fuelled by the vast expansion of global connectivity, facilitated by the Internet, for business and social purposes, which in turn has provided businesses with unprecedented marketing opportunities. New business models are being created based on mathematical formulae that exploit access to and manipulate vast reservoirs of information, which is collected and stored on computers by private corporations and governments.

There have been a number of recent books on digital disruption, but they have focused on the potential uses of disruptive technology, rather than the legal and regulatory dimensions of that technology, or the abuse of it. The subject matter of the book covers a number of topics including how Big Data is feeding innovation, the impact of disruptive technology on copyright law, and how multinational corporations are exploiting new technologies to engage in corporate tax avoidance. There are three cutting edge chapters devoted to a Chinese perspective on digital disruption in relation to Chinese business models, quasi-financial services and digital platforms. The book also has a chapter on virtual currencies, in particular bitcoin, and money laundering risks, as well as a panel discussion on the future of virtual currencies. There are many other topics that we could have included – such as Internet theft, identity and financial privacy, and e-gaming and regulation – that may serve as subjects for a future book.

This book grew out of a conference held at The University of Sydney

Business School on 23 November 2015. This conference provided a holistic view of the opportunities and threats entailed in the digital world of the 21st century. Drawing on specialists in management, computer technology, regulation and the law, the conference provide insights into how digital disruption is impacting businesses, governments, investors and consumers. We are grateful to the many participants at the conference, including Shaoling (Gary) Bai, Mark Gardiner, Arun Kendall, Cindy Nicholson, Kai Riemer, Piers Hogarth-Scott, Robert Thomson, and especially Anthony Wong, who was most helpful in developing the themes of the conference.

We would like to thank the authors of the chapters and various contributors, especially Mary Wyburn and Antony Ting, who are leading researchers and teachers in the Discipline of Business Law at The University of Sydney Business School. We are indebted to many people who have made this book possible, including the initial editorial support of Ms Siew-Ching Lim, as well as Joanne Webb. However, we emphasise that we take ultimate responsibility for any errors in the book.

David Chaikin and Derwent Coshott
Discipline of Business Law
The University of Sydney Business School

Chapter 1

Intellectual Property Law & Disruptive Technology: Focusing on Copyright Law*

Mary Wyburn

Disruptive digital technologies are challenging current business models that are based on existing legal frameworks for the various categories of intellectual property. This chapter discusses one area of intellectual property law, copyright law and its response to disruptive digital technologies. Copyright law has been faced with disruptive digital technologies over a considerable period. In the 1980s the challenge was to bring computer programs within its framework. In 2001, legislative amendments sought to respond to a rapidly developing online digital environment. The chapter looks at Australian case law involving examples of digital disruption affecting several key areas of copyright law: originality, licensing, infringement and defences. It then outlines some further issues falling within these same areas of copyright law that are not yet reflected in the Australian case law.

The various fields of intellectual property law are familiar with the challenges brought by disruptive technologies to business models based on the existing legal frameworks. In recent times disruptive digital technologies have been putting pressure on the current intellectual property law regimes. Patent law, for example, has been grappling with the issue of the registrability of business method patents. Trade mark law has been faced with the use of trade marks as part of domain names, on social networks and as part of online searching and advertising, as well as with copycat and

*This chapter represents the law as at March 2016.

counterfeit products being offered through online auction sites. Copyright law faced disruptive digital technologies at an early stage. In the 1980s, computer technology was brought within the copyright legislative framework in the *Copyright Amendment Act 1984* (Cth). Legislative amendments to address the then emerging online digital environment were implemented in the *Copyright Amendment (Digital Agenda) Act 2000* (Cth).

This chapter focuses on Australian copyright law's response to disruptive digital technologies. It discusses several cases involving digital disruption and its effect on a number of fundamental areas of copyright law: originality and authorship, licensing, infringement and defences. It then discusses some further issues that have been raised in these identified areas of copyright law but which are not yet reflected in the case law.

Recent Australian Copyright Case Law on Digital Disruption

Originality and authorship

The first area of digital disruption of copyright law discussed is that of originality and authorship. A key case is *IceTV v Nine Network Australia*.[1] At first sight the facts of the case appear to reflect a relatively small level of digital disruption. However the decision has had significant consequences for the owners of copyright in commercially valuable compilations of data.

IceTV wanted to include television programmes' title and time information from Nine's weekly television programme schedules, as it appeared in authorised third party aggregated guides, in IceTV's subscription electronic programme guide (EPG) called the 'IceGuide.' The potential for disruption of the existing business model arose from the fact that the EPG was downloadable onto personal video recorders and similar equipment where it would enable recording and then fast forwarding through the advertising that supports the free-to-air television stations. The issue was whether the television programme schedules in question constituted original copyright works, in particular original literary works. The High Court held that copyright originality required some 'independent intellectual effort' meaning originality of the expression of the idea in a material form

---

1 (2009) 239 CLR 458.

and the television programme schedules did not meet the required level of originality.

Before the *IceTV* Case, the accepted view was that copyright originality could only be established where some element of judgment or effort (characterised as 'sweat of the brow') had gone into creating the work, for instance in the compiling of a database of information such as a telephone directory.[2] The finding in the *IceTV* Case meant this was no longer the law. In the subsequent case of *Telstra Corporation Ltd v Phone Directories Company Pty Ltd*,[3] the Full Federal Court denied copyright protection to regional telephone directories (white and yellow pages publications) essentially on the grounds that the works were created not by human authors but were generated by computer software. Applying the *IceTV* decision, the court found that a literary work must be created by a human author who contributes some intellectual effort directed at expressing the idea in a material form.

This leaves the future protection under copyright law of valuable databases compiled through the use of digital technology, rather than human independent intellectual effort, at some risk. There are other potential forms of legal protection for such material, for example under the contract terms on which the rights owner grants access to the material but copyright law no longer operates alongside these other forms of legal protection.

Licensing

Another area of copyright law affected by digital disruption is that of licensing. An illustrative case is *Phonographic Performance Company of Australia Ltd v Commercial Radio Australia Ltd*.[4] It reflects the need for change in current licensing arrangements when users access programming through new digital platforms.

Commercial radio stations, represented by Commercial Radio Australia Ltd (CRA), are currently simulcasting (online streaming) their broadcast programmes. The question in the case was whether that activity

---

2 *Desktop Marketing Systems Pty Ltd v Telstra Corp Ltd* (2002) 192 ALR 433.

3 (2010) 273 ALR 725.

4 (2013) 296 ALR 607.

fell within the terms of the existing contract between CRA and the record company collecting society, the Phonographic Performance Company of Australia Ltd (PPCA). PPCA licenses the use of sound recording copyright material. If the online streaming of broadcast programmes did not fall within the existing contract terms, it would need to be licensed separately.

The current contract referred to the licensing by PPCA of 'broadcasting rights', with 'broadcast' as defined in the *Copyright Act 1968* (Cth). The Act, in s 10, defines broadcast as meaning 'a communication to the public delivered by a broadcasting service within the meaning of the *Broadcasting Services Act 1992*'. The Full Federal Court found that simulcasting was not covered by the current terms of the contract. The CRA and PPCA are now before the Copyright Tribunal seeking the determination of a rate for the licence.

The issue of existing licensing arrangements not covering the newer ways in which copyright material in digital form is accessed by users, has also arisen in respect of compulsory licensing regimes established under the *Copyright Act*. In *Re Audio-Visual Copyright Society Ltd*,[5] the Audio-Visual Copyright Society Ltd (AVCS – known as Screenrights) applied to the Copyright Tribunal to amend the existing Declaration made under s 153F of *Copyright Act*. The declaration provided for Screenrights to be the collecting society for the purposes of Government copying of audio-visual items (i.e. sound recordings, film and television and radio broadcasts, (and works included in them) from a television or radio broadcast (including a broadcast transmitted for a fee) and a television transmission to subscribers to a diffusion service) under Part VII Division 2 of the Act.

The problem was that the declaration was expressed in the technology-specific terms used in the copyright legislation prior to the *Copyright Amendment (Digital Agenda) Act 2000* (Cth). However, the Government was now more frequently accessing the copyright material from the Internet rather than from television or radio. The question was whether the current statutory licensing scheme, providing for Screenrights as the declared collecting society, covered copying that fell within the broader and

5 [2015] ACopyT 4.

technology-neutral 'communication to the public' right introduced by the Digital Agenda amendments. The Copyright Tribunal decided to revoke the existing declaration and make a new declaration that Screenrights be the declared collecting society in relation to Government copying of an audio-visual item made from a communication to the public.

Another key case about the licensing of copyright digital material is *Copyright Agency Ltd v State of NSW*,[6] a case involving the licensing of spatial data. When survey plans (copyright artistic works) are lodged by registered surveyors with the NSW Department of Lands' Lands and Property Information (LPI) division they are imaged electronically and included in LPI's digital database. They are also included in the state's Digital Cadastral Database (DCDB). Copies of the plans are made accessible to Government agencies but they are also licensed by LPI to information brokers and copies of the whole or part of the DCDB are sold by LPI to the public.

Copyright Agency Ltd (CAL), a copyright collecting society, on behalf of its surveyor members, applied to the Copyright Tribunal to determine a rate and terms for the use by Government of the artistic works under ss 183 and 183A of the *Copyright Act* (Crown use provisions) in respect of the copying and communication of the plans to the public. In response, the NSW Government claimed the submission of the plans by the copyright owner (the surveyor) gave rise to an implied licence to use the plans and so no further copyright licence was required.

The High Court found there was no implied licence in favour of the Crown in these circumstances. A rate for the licence was subsequently determined on an application to the Copyright Tribunal in *Copyright Agency Ltd v NSW*.[7]

Infringement

Another important area of copyright faced with issues of digital disruption is that of copyright infringement.

This has been an issue for the newspaper industry, which is facing significant challenges on several digital technology fronts. These include

---

6 (2008) 233 CLR 279.
7 [2013] ACopyT 1.

the growth of news monitoring services and the development of news aggregators – both types of services make use of the news material generated by newspaper organisations. The case of *Fairfax Media Publications Pty Ltd v Reed International Books Australia Pty Ltd*[8] concerned a publisher copying newspaper article headlines (titles) from the Fairfax press and using them in conjunction with abstracts it had made of the newspaper articles. The Federal Court found the newspaper article headlines did not amount to literary works as they were too insubstantial to qualify.

A more significant matter of controversy in the area of copyright infringement has been the potential liability of Internet Service Providers (ISPs). The issue is whether an ISP can be found to be infringing copyright by authorising acts of (primary) copyright infringement by end users, when those end users participate in the sharing of unauthorised copies of copyright material through peer-to-peer file sharing networks such as BitTorrent.

The key case is *Roadshow Films Pty Ltd v iiNet Ltd.*[9] The case was brought by 34 film and television companies (Roadshow) against iiNet Ltd (iiNet) in relation to the infringement of copyright in 86 cinematograph films by way of authorisation of copyright infringement. The High Court found there had been no infringement by way of authorisation by the ISP. For authorisation, the alleged infringer must have power to prevent the primary infringements; it was not enough merely to support or encourage the acts. On the facts presented in the case the ISP had no direct power to prevent its customers using the BitTorrent system to infringe the film copyright.

Faced with the result in the iiNet Case and the failure of copyright owner and ISP groups to reach agreement on a code of conduct for the handling of allegations of copyright infringement, some copyright owners decided to initiate legal proceedings in order to obtain the identity of individual ISP account holders so as to be in a position to take copyright infringement action against them. The preliminary discovery proceedings brought by the rights owners of the film *Dallas Buyers Club* shows that these steps have been controversial.

---

8 (2010) 272 ALR 547.
9 (2012) 248 CLR 42.

In *Dallas Buyers Club LLC v iiNet Ltd*,[10] the copyright rights owners (DBC) applied for preliminary discovery against six ISPs seeking to obtain the identities of account holders that had used 4,726 internet protocol (IP) addresses. The addresses had been identified, through the use of software (Maverik Monitor software), as sharing the copyright film using BitTorrent for which no permission had been granted. The Federal Court ordered the ISPs to provide the names and addresses of the customers associated in their records with the IP addresses.

One of the grounds on which the ISPs had argued against the grant of the application was that it might lead to 'speculative invoicing' by the rights owner. Speculative invoicing occurs where a demand is made for a sum in excess of what might ordinarily be recovered in infringement litigation and it is accompanied by an offer to settle for a smaller sum.[11] In order to address this issue, one of the conditions the court order was made subject to was that the proposed letter to be sent to account holders was to be submitted first to the court.[12] In this way the court could ensure the proper exercise of its discretion to allow the release of the information about the ISP account holders. It could examine the letter in order to determine whether the monetary demands proposed were such that they could 'plausibly be sued for.'[13] In *Dallas Buyers Club LLC v iiNet Ltd (No. 3)*,[14] the preliminary discovery order was stayed until the court had an opportunity to look at the letter DBC was proposing to send to the ISP account holders alleged to have infringed copyright.

DBC then applied to the court to have the stay on the preliminary discovery order lifted. In *Dallas Buyers Club LLC v iiNet Ltd (No. 4)*[15] its application was rejected. The court determined that two of the four heads of damages DBC was proposing to claim in its correspondence with the ISP account holders were not tenable claims. The court indicated it would lift the stay if DBC used the information about subscribers to seek relief

---

10 (2015) 112 IPR 1.

11 *Dallas Buyers Club LLC v iiNet Ltd* (2015) 112 IPR 1, 18 and 19–20.

12 Ibid 22.

13 *Dallas Buyers Club LLC v iiNet (No. 4)* (2015) 114 IPR 297, 299.

14 [2015] FCA 422.

15 (2015) 114 IPR 297.

based on the two permissible heads of damages. However, the court went on to find that because DBC had no presence in Australia, it would be unable to punish DBC for contempt if it failed to honour an undertaking to use the information only in this way, so the court required the undertaking by DBC to be secured by the lodging of a bond of $600,000.[16] A further application by DBC to lift the stay was rejected in *Dallas Buyers Club LLC v iiNet Ltd (No. 5)*.[17] The court ordered that the application for preliminary discovery be dismissed unless further application is made by DBC before a specified date.

Defences

Another important area of copyright law raised by cases involving disruptive digital technology is the defences to copyright infringement. In the case of *National Rugby League Investments Pty Ltd v Singtel Optus Pty Ltd*[18] the owner of the technology was seeking to rely on a defence that was on its face intended to protect an end user.

The National Rugby League (NRL) and the Australian Football League (AFL) own copyright in the films of their football games and the broadcasts of their football games made on free-to-air television. At the relevant time, Telstra Corporation Ltd was the exclusive licensee of these rights owners in relation to Internet and mobile phone platforms.

Singtel Optus Pty Ltd (Optus) introduced its TV Now service. The service enabled a subscriber to click a 'record' button for a programme in an EPG and Optus would then record the programme from the free-to-air television broadcast. For each user four copies were made, one in each of four formats (PC, Apple, Android, 3G) and these were stored on computers in the Optus data centre in Sydney. The subscriber could 'play' the programme in his or her chosen format (it was streamed to the user's device) for 30 days following the original broadcast.

When the NRL and AFL threatened to bring action for copyright infringement, Optus itself commenced action claiming they were ground-

---

16 Ibid 305.
17 [2015] FCA 1437.
18 (2012) 289 ALR 27.

less threats under s 202 of the *Copyright Act*. Optus argued that its TV Now service did not involve any copyright infringement. It claimed that it was the subscribers who made the copies of the programme when they pressed 'record' on the EPG and it was not Optus. Alternatively, it argued that it could rely upon the time shift defence in s 111. The defence allows a copy of a broadcast to be made for private and domestic use in order for the broadcast to be later watched at a more convenient time.

The Full Federal Court found in the circumstances that it was Optus that made the copies or Optus, in concert with the subscriber. It held that the time shift defence did not apply to Optus; there was 'nothing in the language' of the section or its 'provenance' to 'suggest it was intended to cover commercial copying on behalf of individuals.'[19] In the court's view, the 'natural meaning of the section is that the person who makes the copy is the person whose purpose is to use it as prescribed by s 111(1).'[20]

Other Issues of Australian Copyright Law and Digital Disruption

There are a number of other important issues raised by disruptive digital technologies in the areas of copyright law discussed in the previous section of this chapter that are not yet reflected in Australian copyright case law.

One of these issues is determining originality and authorship when data collection is crowdsourced. Crowd science or citizen science uses the enthusiasm of individuals who, after some basic training, contribute to online labour intensive projects requiring human intelligence, rather than computer analysis, to interpret large amounts of data. Those individuals may be experts who want to be involved but there are also lots of amateur enthusiasts keen to contribute to interesting projects. One area in which crowd science has been utilised is the classification of images of galaxies.[21] Another example is the gathering of geographical information, for instance Open Street Map, where volunteers help to map their neighbourhoods and towns.[22]

---

19 *National Rugby League Investments Pty Ltd v Singtel Optus Pty Ltd* (2012) 289 ALR 27, 46.
20 Ibid.
21 Chiara Franzoni and Henry Sauermann, 'Crowd Science: The Organization of Scientific Research in Open Collaborative Projects (2014) 43(1) *Research Policy* 1.
22 T. Scassa and D. Taylor, 'Intellectual Property Law and Geospatial Information: Some

In the case of copyright material created by way of crowdsourced information gathering, the question is whether the contribution of any members of the crowd amounts to copyright authorship in respect of the copyright material. This will in turn affect the ownership of copyright.

Another copyright issue, this time involving the licensing of copyright, arises from the copyright material in digital form generated by individual creators, both amateur and professional, available on social networks (user-generated content). The enormous amount of this material available on online platforms and the potential uncertainty created by the wide range of licensing models adopted in relation to it, has already given rise to litigation overseas.[23] In 2015 there was some press coverage of a matter involving the alleged use of a photograph, and some words accompanying it, that had been posted by a Brisbane teenager on her Instagram account, on part of a t-shirt sold by an activewear brand.[24]

The complexity of licensing arrangements on social networks is further increased by developed and developing user practices on these digital platforms. For instance, on some social platforms the reposting of others' material is part of the practice (e.g. on the Twitter platform, Tweets are re-Tweeted). Another source of licensing complexity is the development, within a brand's marketing activities, of a relationship with individuals who have popular social network accounts and who are actively engaging with the brand.[25] This adds a further layer of complexity to the copyright licensing issues in respect of both the brand's marketing material and the material appearing on the social network account.

The introduction of digital streaming technology is having a profound effect on the way end users are accessing copyright music and film. It is also raising important copyright licensing issues.

Challenges (2014) 6(1) *World Intellectual Property Organisation Journal* 79, 86.

23 For example, *Grauglis v Kappa Map Group LLC* US District Court for the District of Columbia Civil Action No. 14–1043, 18 August 2015, involved a photograph posted to a Flickr page indicated as licensed under one of the Creative Commons licences and used on the front cover of a street atlas.

24 For example, see R Deutrom, 'Fashion Victim', *Courier Mail*, 8 October 2015, 7.

25 C. Low, 'Big Brands Use Follower Force to Drive Sales', *Sydney Morning Herald*, 21 November 2015, 4.

In the case of the streaming of music, there is some concern that despite its popularity, streaming is not generating significant income for recording artists and composers. The streaming platforms have responded by claiming they pay large sums to the rights owners and the problem is how that income from licensing is split between copyright owners of the sound recording and the musical works.[26]

The streaming of movies and television programmes has highlighted another copyright licensing issue, the territoriality of those licensing arrangements. End users are understandably keen to access the widest possible catalogues of streamed digital copyright material but copyright licensing arrangements are generally made on a territorial basis. Consequently the streaming platforms usually incorporate geo-blocking measures (e.g. technology identifying IP addresses so as to reveal the country of origin) to limit the access of their subscribers to material licensed for a particular geographical area. There are indications that a considerable number of subscribers are now making use of virtual private networks (VPNs) to get around geo-blocks. The use of a VPN may be in breach of the contract terms of the streaming service, but whether the use constitutes copyright infringement in some circumstances is controversial.[27] There are recent press reports that one streaming service, Netflix, is intending to take action to prevent its customers from using such measures.[28]

Another important copyright infringement issue is the role of websites containing pirated copyright material. These websites not only make available pirated copyright material for download by others but they also divert online advertising from legitimate websites and generate income for the pirate site operators from advertising placed on the pirate sites.[29]

26 United States Copyright Office, *Copyright and the Music Marketplace: A Report of the Register of Copyrights*, February 2015, III A 1 b, 73–8.

27 See, for example, Australian Copyright Council, *Information Sheet G127v02* (July 2015); Malcolm Turnbull, *Online Copyright Infringement FAQs* <http://www.malcolmturnbull.com.au>.

28 Australian Associated Press, 'US: Netflix to Block Proxy Access to Content', 15 January 2016 <http://www.factiva.com>; C. Griffith, 'Netflix Meets its Match in Blocking Wars', *The Australian*, 22 January 2016, 3.

29 Digital Citizens Alliance, *Good Money Gone Bad: Digital Thieves and the Hijacking of the Online Ad Business* (February 2015); Digital Citizens Alliance, *Good Money Still Going Bad:*

In line with measures already adopted in some overseas jurisdictions (e.g. *Copyright, Designs and Patents Act 1988* (UK) s 97A), the *Copyright Amendment (Online Infringement) Act 2015* (Cth) has been enacted. The legislation enables the Federal Court, on the application by the owner of a copyright, to make an order that a 'carriage service provider' take reasonable steps to disable access to an online location outside Australia that has as its 'primary purpose' to infringe copyright or facilitate the infringement of copyright.[30]

In addition to these infringement issues, there are a number of questions raised about the application of the copyright defences in the context of new digital technologies and digital disruption. For instance, text or data mining technology uses software for the automated searching, extracting and indexing of digital materials (e.g. research journal articles) in order to discover new knowledge or insights, for example patterns not recognised earlier, that can be used to further current research efforts. These processes generally involve copying the whole or part of the data being processed.[31] The question is whether the existing exceptions to copyright infringement would include this activity and, if not, whether it might fall within a wider 'fair use' exception recommended by the Australian Law Reform Commission (ALRC) in its report *Copyright and the Digital Economy*.[32]

Similar questions arise in relation to the caching and indexing activities of search engines using automated web crawlers to locate and index material, including copyright material, on the Internet. Do such activities fall within any of the existing exceptions to copyright infringement, and if not, might they fall within the wider fair use exception recommended in the ALRC report?

An exposure draft of the Copyright Amendment (Disability Access

---

Digital Thieves and the Hijacking of the Online Ad Business (May 2015).

30 Copyright Amendment (Online Infringement) Bill 2015 Explanatory Memorandum, 2. See *Copyright Act 1968* (Cth) s 115A.

31 Jean-Paul Triaille and Jerome de Meeus d'Argenteuil, *Study on the Legal Framework of Text and Data Mining* (De Wolf & Partners, 2014) <http://ec.europa.eu/internal_market/copyright/docs/studies/1403_study2_en.pdf>.

32 Australian Law Reform Commission, *Copyright and the Digital Economy*, Report No. 122 (2013) Ch. 11.

and Other Measures) Bill 2016 (Cth) is currently subject to public consultation. The draft bill includes measures to extend the current 'safe harbour' provisions to include a broader range of online operators such as search engines and cloud storage facilities. The safe harbour provisions limit the types of remedies a copyright owner may obtain against a 'carriage service provider,' in particular they limit monetary remedies in favour of orders to block access, terminate accounts and remove material (*Copyright Act 1968* (Cth) Part V Division 2AA).

Conclusion

The chapter has discussed a number of Australian copyright cases that have addressed the challenges brought by disruptive digital technologies. The cases have highlighted significant issues in key areas of copyright law: originality and authorship, licensing, infringement and defences. The chapter has also discussed other issues that have been raised in these key areas of copyright law but which have yet to reach the courts. These include matters that are the subject of recent legislative changes, for example amendments to address the blocking of pirate websites and proposed legislation intended to extend the safe harbour protections to a wider range of online intermediaries. There is no doubt that the development of new disruptive digital technologies will continue to challenge the area of copyright law but the indications are that the copyright law framework has so far been able to deal with these challenges.

Chapter 2

Big Data Fuels Digital Disruption and Innovation: But Who Owns The Data?

Anthony Wong

A staggering 2.5 quintillion bytes of data are created every day – with 90 per cent of the world's data produced in the last two years alone.[1]

Our economy has been moving from the physical world dominated by tangibles to one motivated by 'bits', 'waves' and 'droplets' of data (intangibles). Correspondingly, the values that define the wealth of our society are also shifting from the tangible to the Digital Economy. The First Industrial Revolution was powered by coal, but as we stand in the midst of the Fourth Industrial Revolution, innovation is now energised by the explosion of data from a myriad of sources.

A high percentage of 'Big Data' is generated by sensors, devices, smart meters and systems collecting transactional data, created largely through computerised and automated processes. Data also includes public and private sector data, and data concerning personal individuals.

With the world increasingly connected by the Internet of Things (IoT),[2] significant disruptions to long-standing business models and beliefs are taking place – from online shopping, connecting and communicating with Uber drivers, musing in driverless cars to transacting with digital

---

1 IBM, *Bringing Big Data to the Enterprise* <http://www-01.ibm.com/software/au/data/bigdata/>.

2 A phrase coined by Kevin Ashton to describe the system where devices are connected through the Internet to transmit, compile and analyse data.

currencies, all powered by data with the aid of applications and networks.

The use of intelligent software in conjunction with the rapid declining cost of digital storage are fuelling the assembly and combination of vast datasets for automated data processing and data mining. The algorithmic software, more cost effective and efficient than human readers, is being progressively deployed across all domains of our society. Data mining will unlock and discover new forms of value, connect previously unseen linkages and provide insights to stimulate growth and innovation in the Digital Economy. Increasingly, copyright and non-copyrightable materials are being used as 'data feed' to 'fuel' text and data analytics.

As our society's dependence on the Digital Economy increases with the rapid evolution of Big Data, it has heightened the issues of 'propertisation' and 'commoditisation' of data. Although the debate on property rights in data is not new, the issue has taken on a renewed emphasis in the context of Big Data. This debate has centred on the ability and freedom to use and extract value from data in the endeavour to ascertain insights to new discoveries, innovation and economic growth.

Protecting value and proprietary rights in Big Data involves a balancing act between many vested interests, including the interests of the 'purported' owner, the 'custodian', the interests of competing third parties, and the interests of the public to access and use data. Many see Big Data as a new commodity – a form of currency – just like spices were in the days of the spice trade in the East.[3]

As identified in the White House report, 'Big Data: Seizing Opportunities, Preserving Values' (White House Big Data Review),[4] data is viewed as a major source of value and economic activity. The report concluded that the explosion of data in today's world can be an unprecedented driver of social progress, but the challenge lies in understanding the many different

---

3 Frank J. Ohlhorst, *Big Data Analytics: Turning Big Data into Big Money* (John Wiley & Sons, 2012); John Lucker, 'Big Data Alchemy: Turn Info Into Money Data Markets', *Information Week (online)*, 13 May 2013 <http://www.informationweek.com/big-data/big-data-analytics/big-data-alchemy-turn-info-into-money/d/d-id/1109933>.
4 Executive Office of the President, 'Big Data: Seizing Opportunities, Preserving Values' (May 2014) 9, <http://www.whitehouse.gov/sites/default/files/docs/big_data_privacy_report_may_1_2014.pdf> (White House Big Data Review).

contexts in which data comes into play including data as property (who owns it), data as a public resource (who manages it and on what principles), and data as identity or as an expression of individual identity.[5]

Economies are starting to form around data, irrespective of whether an adequate legal framework has been built around it. For the most part, traditional intellectual property laws and related rights have proven to be an inadequate solution. These limited interests in data leave out several important rights, which are pertinent in the world of Big Data, including the right to control access, disclosure and use. The debate on data ownership rights has intensified as the use and control of data assets become increasingly critical to our future economies and our ability to innovate – requiring re-balancing of the commercial, private and public interests in data, and not least, privacy concerns.

1. What are the sources and types of Big Data?

An understanding of the sources and types of Big Data is required to properly comprehend the debate on ownership rights in data. Aggregators of Big Data include social media, the web, geospatial data, web-enabled and wearable devices, IoT, sensors, systems capturing transactional data and audit logs.

The convergence of technology and telecommunication have facilitated the proliferation of Internet-enabled device sensors and devices which in turn have provided the base-capacities to collect data from millions of individuals. Personal location data can also come from GPS devices, cell-tower triangulation of mobile devices, mapping of wireless networks and in-person payments.

Data comes in various forms and includes public and private sector information, and data about personal individuals. Public Sector Information (PSI) comprises the largest subset of Big Data and may consist of research data, public registers, train and transport timetables and administrative data from federal, state and local authorities.[6]

---

5 Ibid 3. The report referred to a quote by Professor Sheila Jasanoff, Harvard Professor of Science & Technology Studies.
6 For further information, refer to the European Commission Directorate General for the Information Society, 'Commercial Exploitation of Europe's Public Sector Infor-

PSI is created based on specific laws and regulations and includes company registers, intellectual property registers, land and titles information, land survey and geospatial data, vehicle registers, population and census data. Such data has traditionally been used by institutions of government for public and government administration and policy-making. With the advent of Big Data and open access facilitated by Internet and cloud technologies, it may now be readily available to the private sector. However, release of PSI may be restricted due to privacy and security concerns and other overriding public interest against disclosure. Access to PSI is typically regulated by statutes but may also be accessible on the basis of Freedom of Information laws.[7]

Private sector information includes datasets containing customer lists, transactional information covering a spectrum of financial, payment, purchasing (both offline and online) and service transactions.

As described in the report by the US President's Council of Advisors of Science & Technology, some data is 'born digital, created specifically for digital use by a device or data processing system.'[8]

History will see the Big Data revolution as disruptive and another big game-changer since the invention of the printing press and the Internet, challenging centuries-old business models. In the world of Big Data, these datasets could be created, collected and obtained (sometimes even verified) automatically or as a secondary by-product of another business enterprise. Some will require the investments of time, capital and labour, while others may only require computing processing time. It all comes down to the types and forms of datasets, how they are derived and the purpose they serve.

The challenge is, should some of these datasets be publicly available, or should some producers of capital and labour-intensive datasets be able to inhibit and restrict access to these datasets from data mining and analysis and to safeguard their ability to recoup their investments?

---

mation – Executive Summary' (2000) <ftp://ftp.cordis.europa.eu/pub/econtent/docs/2000_1558_en.pdf>.

7 See Thomson Reuters, *New South Wales Administrative Law* (at 25 April 2016) [50.120]. See also Thomson Reuters, *Federal Administrative Law* (at 25 April 2016) [FOI.0.10].

8 White House Big Data Review, above n 4.

The structure of the chapter

This chapter explores ownership interests in data assets in the era of Big Data and goes beyond intellectual property law. As discussed by Nimmer,[9] it includes rights developed in areas of law not commonly viewed as property in our law regimes.

In writing this chapter I have been taken on a journey, and sharing Merges' sentiments in the opening pages of his book,[10] it is perhaps a longer journey than anticipated. Evolving property law to the next level to parallel the challenges posed by Big Data – taking the evolutionary steps from real property to embrace intellectual property, and then to Big Data, is perhaps over-stretching the traditional concepts of property law; it definitely has 'the feel of a northern fir in the tropics, or a damp fern in the high desert.'[11]

However, I take comfort in the words of Nimmer, 'We deal here with a major, transformative phenomenon. We do not need to capture the Genie into a single, confined bottle in order to discuss its consequences in our lives and in the life of the law.'[12]

This chapter takes up one of the challenges identified in the White House report – Big Data as property (who owns it); and the layered complexities and issues pertaining to the granting of property rights in data. In its relentless 'technological progress', the Big Data phenomenon has overtaken the slow march of our law and has embraced and encapsulated some of the facets of our concepts of property without giving due regard and serious thought to the implications of treating data as property. In an attempt to create order from a run-away phenomenon, this chapter will review whether there should be underlying policy reasons for according some form of property rights in the context of Big Data, and if not some 'bundles of rights'.

In Section 2, we review the state of play of property rights in data and the legal and economic structures that define ownership of data.

---

9 Raymond T. Nimmer, Thomson Reuters, *Information Law* (7 June 2014) [2:1].
10 Robert P. Merges, *Justifying Intellectual Property* (Harvard University Press, 2011) 4.
11 Ibid.
12 Nimmer, above n 9, [1:8].

In Section 3, we explore the challenges posed by data ownership; and in Section 4 we briefly outline the concept of control versus ownership.

This chapter does not purport to resolve all of the issues that relate to Big Data and property rights, but provides a starting base for understanding some of the emerging challenges of ownership and control of data. It will touch on but not cover in any detail the traditional bases for intellectual property protection of information such as copyright, patent and the quasi-intellectual property doctrines under confidential information and trade secrets. These areas have already been exhaustively covered elsewhere.

2. State of play on property rights in data (including economics of data) in the context of Big Data

In a study of the economic value of open data, the McKinsey Global Institute determined that government data could unlock more than US $3 trillion in value every year in seven domains of the global economy: education, transportation, consumer products, electricity, oil and gas, health care and consumer finance.[13]

The EU Commission has also launched an Open Data Strategy for Europe, which is expected to deliver a €40 billion boost to the EU's economy each year.[14]

To fully appreciate the economics of Big Data, we should begin by exploring its benefits.

What are the benefits of Big Data?

Data's value lies in its use, not its mere possession.[15] Big Data tools allow us to combine, interrogate, mine and analyse large structured or unstruc-

---

13 McKinsey Global institute, *Open Data: Unlocking Innovation and Performance with Liquid Information* (2013) <http://www.mckinsey.com/insights/business_technology/open_data_unlocking_innovation_and_performance_with_liquid_information>.
14 European Commission, '*Digital Agenda*: Turning Government Data into Gold' (Press Release, 12 December 2011) <http://ec.europa.eu/digital-agenda/en/news/turning-government-data-gold>.
15 Viktor Mayer-Schonberger and Kenneth Cukier, *Big Data: A Revolution That Will Transform How We Live, Work, and Think* (Eamon Dolan/Houghton Mifflin Harcourt, 2013) 122.

tured, multiple datasets[16] with ease where the sum of these datasets is more valuable than its parts; allowing us to identify correlations that were not easily done previously. It is a competitive advantage to find new ways to interpret data and process them faster using Big Data analytics: 'just as with gold, it is through mining that one finds the nuggets of value that can affect the bottom line.'[17]

Big Data, including data about individuals, also has value in the marketplace – our age, sex, genes, where we live, ethnicity, education, what we do for a living, our financial and transaction records, our beliefs, preferences, purchasing and lifestyle habits – all provide correlation data as to the products and services that we might be interested in, providing valuable data for targeted dollars and marketing.

The roles of institutions are also changing as we clamour for ever-greater productivity and efficiency. In their endeavours to comply with money laundering legislation, including the 'Knowing your customer' requirements, financial institutions have discovered that they have been sitting on a gold mine of data about their customers including:

- Where they shop;
- What they buy and their favourite restaurants; and
- Where they go for holidays.

This facilitates their move to provide new 'non-financial' services including travel and car insurance by partnering with traditional and non-traditional players.

Similarly, telecommunications providers have been collecting data as part of their 'normal' business enterprise including our:

- Service payment transactions and our service usage plans;
- Movements and places where we visit – using the geo-location tracking abilities in our mobile devices; and
- Subscriber content and viewing habits,

---

16 In addition, data, in its raw form, is now also available for analysis, in contrast with traditional structured databases.

17 Ohlhorst, above n 3, 19.

Which facilitates their ability to promote targeted marketing products and services based on our geo-location.

Much of the value of Big Data may be derived from the secondary uses of data, rather than its normal or primary use.

Big Data also challenges existing privacy frameworks and principles including the definition of personal information, principles of data minimisation, purpose limitation and the concept of consent.

Many recent commentators are of the view that anonymisation or de-identification is not robust enough against future re-identification techniques that are being developed for many legitimate applications of Big Data.[18] Big Data allows us to data mine, analyse and create profiles on individuals easier than at any time in the past.

Although many scholars from the American, English and European traditions have advocated for the recognition of property rights in personal information, the law is reluctant to accept the existence of fully-fledged proprietary interests in data as such.[19]

This chapter does not cover property rights in personal information in any detail. The subject of property rights in personal information is complex and deserves a chapter in its own right. Numerous authors have covered this subject exhaustively, including Patricia Mell in her paper, 'Seeking Shade in a Land of Perpetual Sunlight: Privacy as Property in the Electronic Wilderness'[20] and also Vera Bergelson, 'It's Personal but Is It Mine? Toward Property Rights in Personal Information'.[21]

Hemnes, in his analysis on the subject,[22] questions whether 'identity theft' laws have endowed some form of proprietary interests in personal

18 President's Council of Advisors on Science and Technology, 'Big Data and Privacy: A Technological Perspective' (1 May 2014) 38, <http://www.whitehouse.gov/sites/default/files/microsites/ostp/PCAST/pcast_big_data_and_privacy_-_may_2014.pdf>.
19 Maurizio Borghi and Stavroula Karapapa, *Copyright and Mass Digitization: A Cross-Jurisdictional Perspective* (Oxford University Press, 2013) 147.
20 Patricia Mell, 'Seeking Shade in a Land of Perpetual Sunlight: Privacy as Property in the Electronic Wilderness' (1996) 11(1) *Berkeley Technology Law Journal*.
21 Vera Bergelson, 'It's Personal but Is It Mine? Toward Property Rights in Personal Information' (2003) 37(2) *UC Davis Law Review* 379, 412.
22 Thomas Hemnes, 'The Ownership and Exploitation of Personal Identity in the New Media Age' (2012) 12(1) *John Marshall Review of Intellectual Property Law* 29.

information: 'If something is capable of being stolen, and if one can remedy the theft, does this not imply that it was owned in the first place?'[23] He concluded that there are certainly forces pushing in that direction, but it has not happened yet and suggested that in a future period, personal information in one's digital identity 'will have grown into something closer to a property right in one's identity.'[24]

Most jurisdictions in Australia have enacted legislation in relation to identity theft.[25]

The statutory provisions may have countered the threat of identity theft but it has not enlightened us or justified the basis of the protection using any property law concepts behind the 'thing' – the identity, that is capable of being stolen.

Notions of property and data

The foundation of our Australian legal system is property law and even in the 21st century, ownership of and property rights are still of paramount concern. The law of property has developed over centuries, originally for the purpose of protecting interests in land and, relatively recently, interests in other things where rights of ownership may be exerted such as goods, and intangible properties (e.g. rights under intellectual property.

Property rights evolve and change to address certain practical needs of a given epoch in our society. Those needs change alongside our changing values and norms. Literature abounds on the different senses in which the term 'property' has been used to encapsulate the move from the traditional notions of property, such as land and chattels, to the notion of property in intangibles. We are embarking on yet another significant leap, this time specifically, property or 'property-like' considerations in Big Data.

It is difficult to define property with any precision as the 'notions of property inevitably change to reflect their context.'[26] Property deals with

---

23 Ibid.

24 Ibid.

25 See, eg., *Law and Justice Legislation Amendment (Identity Crimes and Other Measures) Act 2011* (Cth); *Criminal Code Act 1995* (Cth); *Crimes Amendment (Fraud, Identity and Forgery Offences) Act 2009* (NSW).

26 Beverley-Smith Huw, *The Commercial Appropriation of Personality* (Cambridge University Press, 2002) 286.

rights, and if recognised under established heads of law are claims 'good against the world', often described as 'rights to exclude others'.[27]

Data is another dimension to the intangible properties such as rights under intellectual property. Data shares a number of characteristics with intellectual property including the following:

- It may be contained in a tangible medium like paper, document, DVD, computer, device or tape.
- It cannot be physically possessed.
- The same data may be included in many different products.
- It may be the copyrightable work itself as contained in an expression.
- It may be the confidential information subject to secrecy or confidential arrangements.
- Data may be contained in a patent.
- The provision, use or transfer of data does not exhaust it in the true real property sense.

Protection by existing intellectual property and related rights

Existing laws in relation to copyright, patent, confidential information and trade secrets, and trademark, all relate to and protect rights involving information.

As observed by Nimmer, 'copyright law has become a primary source of property rights in information in the 1990s.'[28] However, copyright is not an adequate framework for the consideration of property rights in all droplets of data as it only provides owners with a limited property right in the expression of the information.[29] Copyright law does not concern itself with the control or flow of ideas, facts or data per se. The data components contained in the copyrighted work may not be protected, no matter how valuable. Ideas and facts are generally regarded to be in the public domain.[30]

---

27 See Merges, above 10, 100.
28 Nimmer, above n 9, [2:8].
29 The nature of the copyright in a literary, dramatic or musical work is defined under the *Copyright Act 1968* (Cth) s 31.
30 See Pamela Samuelson, 'Is Information Property?' (1991) 34(3) *Communications of the ACM* 16.

The *Copyright Act 1968* (Cth) has been expanded and extended to cover technological protection devices that control access to copyright material.[31] However, they leave out important rights, which are pertinent in the world of Big Data, including the right to control and use, except to the extent provided by the exclusive rights under the *Copyright Act*.[32]

There is currently much debate around the very concept of 'use' as illustrated by the long-running Google Books litigation where US federal Judge Chin ruled that the Google Books project is within the bounds of US copyright law.[33] Google had not secured permission from copyright owners to digitise their books and/or to display short 'snippets' of surrounding text in relation to the search term online.

Borghi, in his analysis of the concept of use in copyright, suggests that it 'involves various kinds of activities, some of which are free for anyone to carry out – reading, listening to, or viewing a work and enjoying it, learning from it, and building upon it – and some others are reserved for the author.'[34] In the context of Google Books, he added that the:

> Technological transformative uses, by contrast, include activities where the work is no longer used as a work but as something else – for instance, as a carrier of data to feed information into computers. This is what we call, using an umbrella term, automated text processing.[35]

It is unlikely that the 'technological transformative uses' and the large-scale digitisation by Google in the US would be supported under current Australian copyright law. As suggested by Nimmer, 'It is also true that copyright does not generally create any right to prevent others from using or disclosing the facts or expression to others if this occurs without

---

31 *Copyright Act 1968* (Cth) ss 116AN, 116AO and 116AP.
32 Australian Law Reform Commission, *Copyright and the Digital Economy*, Report No. 122 (2013) Ch. 11 ('Incidental or Technical Use and Data and Text Mining'), which deals with, and advocates for, fair use or dealing for text and data mining for non-commercial research and non-consumptive use. <http://www.alrc.gov.au/publications/copyright-report-122>.
33 *Authors Guild Inc v Google Inc.*, 954 F.Supp.2d 282 (S.D.N.Y. 2013).
34 Borghi & Karapapa, *Copyright and Mass Digitization: A Cross-Jurisdictional Perspective*, 45.
35 Ibid.

copying the expression.'[36]

The right to control the use of information may also arise under patent law or other laws. Patent law protects the use of ideas or information contained in the patent, by restricting the practice of the invention for a period of time.

In Australia and elsewhere, whether information can be properly characterised as property in the context of confidential information, has been subjected to much academic and judicial commentary over the last half century.[37]

However, if the owner of the confidential information places it in the public domain and accessible for 'Big Data' mining and analysis, the inherent 'secrecy' may be lost.

Confidential information is sometimes described as having a proprietary character, not because property is the rational basis of protection, but because of the effect of equitable protection.[38] In Australia, as in the United Kingdom, there is authority supporting the proposition that information is not property.[39]

3. Challenges to the current concepts of Data Ownership

The rapid emergence of Big Data and our society's dependence on the Digital Economy have heightened the debate on our ability and freedom to use and extract value from data, compilations and datasets without fear of prosecution in the endeavour to achieve new insights, discoveries, innovation and growth.

Granting separate property rights to datasets would create a substantial barrier to the evolution of Big Data and our ability to mine valu-

---

36 See Raymond T. Nimmer and Patricia Ann Krauthaus, 'Information as a Commodity: New Imperatives of Commercial Law' (1992) 55 *Law and Contemporary Problems* 115.

37 For an introduction to the protection of Information using the law of confidential information, see Lahore, LexisNexis, *Patents, Trade Marks & Related Rights* (25 April 2016) [30,000].

38 Ibid [30,020].

39 See, eg., *Federal Commissioner of Taxation v United Aircraft Corp* (1943) 68 CLR 525, 534; *Moorgate Tobacco Co Ltd v Philip Morris Ltd (No. 2)* (1984) 156 CLR 414, 438; *Breen v Williams* (1996) 186 CLR 71, 81, 90, 111, 125; and *Australian Broadcasting Corporation v Lenah Game Meats Pty Ltd* (2001) 208 CLR 199, 271.

able gems from these datasets.

In the world of Big Data, these datasets could be created, collected and obtained (sometimes even verified) automatically or as a by-product of another business enterprise. Some will require the investments of time, capital and labour, while others may only require computing processing time. It all comes down to the types and forms of datasets, how they are derived and the purpose they serve.

The different types and forms of Big Data have challenged and will continue to challenge our thinking and concepts around the question of data ownership. It has also created uncertainty in the boundaries of control and data ownership.

Rights in data come in many forms and from a variety of sources. For the most part, traditional intellectual property law has proven to be inadequate to provide protection.[40] The traditional intellectual property regimes do not provide adequate cover for data and information-based products sufficiently well. Indeed, these laws would exclude most of the Big Data datasets (in whole or in part) from protection.

A large percentage of Big Data datasets (including outputs from device sensors, mobile and GPS devices, smart meters, and systems collecting transactional data) created through a largely computerised and automated process will suffer serious hurdles in securing copyright protection and will probably not have sufficient authorial contribution for copyright to subsist.

In addition, due to the dynamic nature of some Big Data databases, a number of contributors, researchers, analysts and programmers could also be involved. As showed in *IceTV Pty Ltd v Nine Network Australia Pty Ltd*,[41] and *Telstra Corp Ltd v Phone Directories Co Pty Ltd*,[42] there could be difficulties in identifying authors where a work is created and updated over time by a large number of people and using automated processes which

---

40 See Kristen Osenga, 'Information May Want to Be Free, But Information Products Do Not: Protecting and Facilitating Transactions in Information Products' (2009) 30(5) *Cardozo Law Review* 2099, 2101.

41 *IceTV Pty Ltd v Nine Network Australia Pty Ltd* (2009) 239 CLR 458.

42 *Telstra Corp Ltd v Phone Directories Co Pty Ltd* (2010) 194 FCR 142. The High Court refused to grant Telstra special leave to appeal the decision of the Full Federal Court.

lack authorial contribution.

In *Phone Directories*, Gordon J found that none of the 'authors' exercised 'independent intellectual effort' or 'sufficient effort of a literary nature' in creating the phone directories[43] and emphasised that the authorship/originality nexus is important in subsistence of copyright.[44]

The current copyright regime does not protect facts, compilations/databases generated by computers with little or no authorial input or insufficient 'originality' as illustrated in *IceTV* and *Phone Directories*.

Many datasets or databases that are by-products (i.e. secondary) of an organisation's main activities (such as airlines schedules, stock market data, member directories, box scores, real estate listings and results of scientific experiments) would probably not receive protection, unless there is sufficient 'originality' to meet the threshold enunciated in *IceTV* and *Phone Directories*.

Although sufficiency of 'originality' for copyright protection in a form of expression is a matter of fact and degree,[45] the author/originality correlation poses great challenges for those seeking to protect Big Data datasets, which are created or collected with little or no authorial involvement. In fact, most Big Data aspirants strive for data comprehensiveness over selectivity.

Using vast computing resources and power including cloud computing, algorithmic programs are more cost effective and efficient (both in time and money) during data mining and analysis in identifying trends and correlation in Big Data. These algorithmic programs may have been imbued with the requisite selective logic by their programmers, which effectively replace the use of human authors in the selection, identification, verification and presentation of the expressed output.

In *Phone Directories*, Gordon J found that there was no relevant 'intellectual effort' by Telstra's employees or contractors in understanding or applying the rules, which determines the form of expression of the phone directories (Rule). While the relevant 'intellectual effort' was expended

---

43 *Telstra Corporation Ltd v Phone Directories Pty Ltd* [2010] FCA 44, [340].
44 Ibid [344].
45 *IceTV Pty Ltd v Nine Network Australia Pty Ltd* [2009] HCA 14, [99]; *Telstra Corporation Ltd v Phone Directories Pty Ltd* [2010] FCA 44, [25] and [26].

on the computer systems and the development[46] of the Rules[47] used to generate the phone directories and was anterior to the phone directories taking its material form, her Honour was not prepared to carry through the 'intellectual effort' expended on the computer systems and the development of the Rules to the phone directories. The authorship/originality nexus was broken.

Without legislative reform, our 19th century copyright concepts of authorship and fixation, will pose challenges for those seeking to protect their datasets in the era of Big Data. Unless the law is amended, investments in a large percentage of Big Data datasets will be left without effective protection. However, the lack of protection for Big Data datasets would be beneficial for those advocating in favour of narrower ownership rights in data.

Issues pertaining to Computer Generated databases and datasets

Commentators have long distinguished between computer-assisted[48] and computer-generated works. Under current Australian law, the former category posed few copyright problems, but computer-generated Big Data datasets with little or no human intervention would be a stumbling block to copyright's subsistence.

Using the reasoning of Gordon J in *Phone Directories*, an algorithm written for Big Data mining and analysis by a separate person from the one executing the algorithm would break the authorship/originality nexus, resulting in no protection for the selected dataset produced from the data mining and analysis.[49]

Our courts have taken a rather literal and technical approach in the

46 *Telstra Corporation Ltd v Phone Directories Pty Ltd* [2010] FCA 44, [165].

47 The Rules determine the form of expression of the phone directories and where human discretion was exercised, it was dictated by the Rules. See *Telstra Corporation Ltd v Phone Directories Pty Ltd* [2010] FCA 44, [162]–[166].

48 Here the computer is used as a tool, equivalent to the painter's brush or the writer's pen by the author in the creation of the work.

49 See the statement by Gordon J: 'the person or persons who utilise the Rules and who, therefore, are submitted by the Applicants to be authors of the Works, do not exercise either 'independent intellectual effort' or 'sufficient effort of a literary nature' to be considered an author within the meaning of the Copyright Act': *Telstra Corporation Ltd v Phone Directories Pty Ltd* [2010] FCA 44, [162].

IceTV and *Phone Directories* cases in relation to the roles and uses of computers and their equivalency to the painter's brush or the writer's pen in the creation of the databases by the author. It may be unfortunate for some that the courts' focus was on the 'last step in the creative process and then look for an immediate, direct link to a computer or human in order to determine authorship'[50] without taking a wider view of the whole creative process.

The UK has implemented specific provisions to protect computer-generated work.[51] Section 9(3) of the UK *Copyright Designs and Patents Act 1988* provides that 'in the case of a literary, dramatic, musical or artistic work which is computer-generated, the author shall be taken to be the person by whom the arrangements necessary for the creation of the work were undertaken'.

Despite the recommendations of the Copyright Law Review Committee[52] and the Copyright Law Review Committee[53] to adopt the UK's approach, no legislative changes have been undertaken by the Australian Government, resulting in a situation whereby the wider use of technology will hinder the securing of copyright protection in compilations and datasets, including in computer-generated works. Perhaps that is a blessing in disguise for the proponents of the information commons.

There is also no *sui generis* database right in Australia, such as in the EU Database Directive in the EU.

In the era of Big Data, rights to control access, disclosure, use and the ability to extract value from data are paramount. With the advances in

---

50 Lief Gamertsfelder, *Corporate Information and the Law* (LexisNexis Australia, 2013) 40 [2.47].

51 Section 178 of the UK *Copyright Designs and Patents Act 1988* defines 'computer-generated work' to mean work 'generated by computer in circumstances such that there is no human author of the work'. Similar provisions have been replicated in New Zealand, Ireland, India, Hong Kong and South Africa. The US, while not having enacted similar provisions, has been able to better protect computer-generated work.

52 The Copyright Law Review Committee (CLRC) in 1995 released its report on copyright and computer software. The report included a section on computer-generated works.

53 See paragraphs 5.45 and 5.46 of the report by the Copyright Law Review Committee, *Simplification of the Copyright Act 1968, Part 2 – Categorisation of Subject Matter and Exclusive Rights, and other Issues* Commonwealth of Australia (1999).

technology and the rapid proliferation of cloud and Internet technologies, wholesale reproduction or copying as a step in the process of data mining and analysis may be a thing of the past. Big Data tools are now coming to maturity that will allow the combination, interrogation, mining and analysis of large structured or unstructured, multiple datasets with ease, and without the need to undertake wholesale reproduction or copying as a requisite step.

4. The Concept of Control versus Ownership

In the era of Big Data, the right to control access to the data contained in a system can often be more important than the right to control copying of the data.

Nimmer, in his paper, expanded the concept of control: 'The right to control another's access to information can implicate several distinct bodies of law, including the law of trade secrets, criminal law, communications law, and various laws relating to privacy interests.'[54] Copyright also plays a role. In the context of privacy law, the concept of control commonly referred to as 'notice and consent' is illusory in the world of Big Data.

I provide two examples below to illustrate the complexities inherent to the question of ownership and control of information.

Example 1 – Unauthorised Access to Data

Computer crime laws treat unauthorised access to computer systems in a manner analogous to trespass. The concepts commonly associated with the law of torts and property – the action for trespass to land (real property) and to chattels have been extended to protect data in the computer environment by a number of state and federal statutory criminal provisions in Australia. Rights to control access to information are found in the Australian federal cybercrime provisions: in the *Criminal Code 1995* (Criminal Code) and in the equivalent state provisions.[55]

The Criminal Code establishes a computer system as a protected environment and creates a crime analogous to trespass to a person's home for

---

54 See Nimmer and Krauthaus, above n 36, 118.
55 Australia adopted the Council of Europe Convention on Cybercrime on 1 March 2013.

unauthorised access. Even if no direct harm occurs, s 478.1(1) recognises that the provider of the protected computer system has an inherent right to exclude unauthorised access to data held and restricted by an access control system associated with a function of the computer.

The access control right in s 478.1(1) requires the presence of an 'access control system associated with a function of the computer'– i.e. a protected zone or environment. As in trespass to land, the section also requires that the act of unauthorised access to the data held in a computer be intentional. However, there is no requirement that the data be confidential in character or be owned by the provider of the protected computer system.

The above is an example of government intervention using a statutory framework to protect proprietary interest (the data) in a digital environment, without the requirement to establish ownership in the data held and restricted by an access control system associated with a function of the computer.

The right accorded by the *Criminal Code* is a claim 'good against the world' providing a 'right to exclude others' and is strikingly similar to what the provider of the protected computer system would have enjoyed if they owned the data in the protected computer system.

In addition, the *Copyright Act* may also be invoked if the 'access control system'– technological protection devices that control access to the copyright material – has been circumvented.[56]

Example 2 – Personally Controlled Electronic Health Records

One of the areas that will greatly benefit from Big Data is health care. Using Big Data tools to combine, interrogate, mine and analyse large structured or unstructured and multiple datasets, one would have the ability to identify correlations in health data to discover a cure for a disease, sickness or to improve medical knowledge.

The Australian Government's personally controlled electronic health (eHealth) record system[57] was launched on 1 July 2012 utilising the framework provided by the *Personally Controlled Electronic Health Re-*

---

56 *Copyright Act 1968* (Cth) ss 116AN, 116AO and 116AP.
57 See, Department of Health, Australian Government, *Welcome to My Health Record*

cords Act 2012 (Cth) ('PCEHR Act').

People seeking healthcare in Australia (Patient) can register for an eHealth record – a secure, electronic summary of their health information such as prescribed medications, allergies and treatments that they have received. The eHealth record system gives the Patient control over their health information, and they can choose to 'opt-out' at any time. The Patient controls who has access to his or her eHealth record, what information others can see and what records are uploaded by establishing access controls on his or her eHealth record.

Certain documents may be marked as 'Restricted Access' by the Patient, and the Patient may provide the 'Restricted Access' code to the healthcare providers they want to have access to the 'Restricted Access' documents in his or her eHealth Record. The Patient may also control the level of read and write access to his or her eHealth record by each healthcare provider.

The above implementation of the personally controlled electronic health record system poses many legal questions.

At the CeBIT's eHealth conference in Sydney in May 2014, Professor Morgan[58] raised concern about the issue of ownership and control of the personally controlled electronic health record system.

Are we able to mine the personally controlled electronic health record system for the 'nuggets of gold' that could uncover the cause of a particular disease, a cure for a sickness or a particular lifestyle that might trigger a certain illness?

Medical practitioners in Australia have fiercely guarded their ownership and control over their patient records. The High Court in the case of

---

<http://www.ehealth.gov.au/internet/ehealth/publishing.nsf/content/home>; and Office of the Australian Information Commissioner, *My Health Records* <http://www.oaic. gov.au/privacy/privacy-act/e-health-records>.

58 Professor Kenneth Morgan, special advisor to the Vice-Chancellor of Flinders University on cyber-security and resilience, discussed the future of e-health at CeBIT's eHealth conference in Sydney in May 2014. As reported by Cynthia Karena, 'Ownership of Patient Records, Just One Challenge in E-Health', *Sydney Morning Herald (online)*, 7 May 2014, <http://www.smh.com.au/it-pro/government-it/ownership-of-patient-records-just-one-challenge-in-ehealth-20140507-zr66p.html>.

Breen v Williams[59] established that patients have no proprietary rights or interests in the information contained in their own medical records.

The conclusion was based on the purpose for which the medical record was created, as well as the nature of the particular relationship between the patient and the health care professional. The High Court concluded that a medical record is ordinarily created by medical practitioners or healthcare providers for their own professional purposes in order to provide health care services to the patient, including diagnosis, treatment and advice. As the creation of medical records is not generally a term of any contractual relationship between a patient and the medical practitioner or healthcare provider, medical records, as a general rule, are the property of the medical practitioner or the healthcare providers that created them.

However, the law has not granted medical practitioners and health-care providers exclusive rights to patient information. Medical practitioners and healthcare providers owe their patients a legal and ethical duty not to use or disclose personal health information without their patient's consent unless a legal obligation or recognised exception exists.[60]

The *PCEHR Act* provides access by patients to their records uploaded onto the system, although ownership of the original record (statute or contract apart) is still presumably vested in the person who has created the record. The PCEHR Act is silent on the question of information ownership and property rights.

The *PCEHR Act* imposes limits on the collection, use and disclosure of health information included in the eHealth record. Pre-existing privacy laws at federal, state and territory levels also apply to protect information held about individuals; to allow them access to such information; as well as to determine whether it is accurate and collected for appropriate purposes.[61] Rights of access also exist under Freedom of Information legislation,

---

59 *Breen vWilliams* (1996) 186 CLR 71, 88–90, Dawson and Toohey J.J. expressed the view, in the context of the information in medical records, that there 'can be no proprietorship in information as information, because once imparted, belongs equally to both the patient and the health professional.'
60 For a general discussion of the legal duty of confidentiality owed by medical practitioners, see LexisNexis, *Halsbury's Laws of Australia* (at 12 April 2011) [280-4000].
61 *Privacy Act 1988* (Cth) extends the rights of access to documents held by private and

which provides patients with a statutory right of access to their personal health records held by public authorities.[62]

Although the ownership of the original eHealth record may vest in the medical practitioner or healthcare provider who has created it, the above example illustrates the many layers of rights, controls and obligations that exist in relation to the information held in the eHealth record.

The *PCEHR Act* introduces new legal issues adding to the many existing issues as the records are held by a third party who operates the shared health record infrastructure (SEHR). There are questions as to whether the collation of records in a database by the SEHR conveys some proprietary rights (including copyright) to the infrastructure owner, over and above the copyright in the opinion provided by the medical practitioner or health care provider. There are also legal questions as to which organisation would be responsible for satisfying freedom of information requests for information in the shared record.

Treating patient data as private property would hamper the creation of Big Data datasets, even in an anonymised and de-identified form. It would be costly and laborious to secure rights to individual records, as one of the benefits from Big Data is the ability to combine, interrogate, mine and analyse large structured or unstructured, and multiple datasets to identify correlations to discover a cure for a disease, sickness or other information to improve medical knowledge.

We will have to wait and see whether our government, with the appropriate protective measures and safeguards to ensure confidentiality and privacy, would be open at a future period to allow data mining and analysis of the personally controlled electronic health record system.

Commonwealth public sector health providers. Also see *Health Records (Privacy and Access) Act 1997* (ACT), *Health Records and Information Privacy Act 2002* (NSW), *Health Records Act 2001* (NSW). There are no equivalent provisions in the other jurisdictions.

62 *Freedom of Information Act 1982* (Cth) s 11. This legislation only has effect on agencies or organisations which are under the control of the Commonwealth; *Freedom of Information Act 1989* (ACT) s 10; *Government Information (Public Access) Act 2009* (NSW) s 3; *Right to Information Act 2009* (QLD) s 23; *Freedom of Information Act 1991* (SA) s 12; *Right to Information Act 2009* (TAS) ss 3, 7; *Freedom of Information Act 1982* (VIC) s 13; *Freedom of Information Act 1992* (WA) s 10.

Conclusion

What are the possible ownership constructs/model for data in the era of Big Data?

The White House Big Data Review advocates for increased clarity on the question of ownership and property rights in Big Data. This matter should be high on our legislative agenda. However, we should tread with caution, as this chapter illustrates the layered complexities and issues pertaining to the granting of ownership rights in all data – especially data not currently embraced by our existing laws in relation to copyright, patent, confidential information and trade secrets. Defining ownership in the context of Big Data involves a balancing act between many vested interests including the interests of the purported owner, the interests of competing third parties and the interests of the public to have access to, and use of, the data.

From example 2 in Section 4, it would appear that the framework of patient entitlements and protections afforded by the *PCEHR Act,* together with the myriads of privacy legislation (both state and federal) are remarkably similar to what patients would enjoy if they owned their eHealth information. The collective effect of these layered entitlements and protections may sometimes resemble the 'bundle of rights' in property law. This similarity suggests that property rights seem less appropriate and perhaps, 'should not be readily transferred and applied to more modern forms of wealth.'[63]

Has Big Data Changed Our Perspective of Property Rights in Information? I believe it has. The average man or woman in our society would be surprised to discover that data in their possession, and in their computer or device, might not be owned by them in the traditional sense.

The *Criminal Code* recognises that the provider of the protected computer system has an inherent right to exclude unauthorised access to data, and is strikingly similar to what the provider of the protected computer system would have enjoyed if they owned the data in the protected

---

63 T.C. Grey, 'The Disintegration of Property' in J.R. Pennock and J.W. Chapman (eds.), *Nomos XXII: Property* (New York University Press, 1980) 78. See also, S.R. Munzer, *A Theory of Property* (Cambridge University Press, 1990) 31–6.

computer system.

In addition, Hemnes questions whether identity theft laws have endowed some form of proprietary interests in personal information:

> If something is capable of being stolen, and if one can remedy the theft, does this not imply that it was owned in the first place?[64]

We need a model for managing data. The White House Big Data Review suggests a model for the development of a set of tags to encode data:

> Tagging both enables precise access control and preserves links to source data and the purpose of its original collection. The end result is a taxonomy of rules governing where information goes and tracking where it came from and under what authority.[65]

Big Data is created, derived and collected from a myriad of sources comprising droplets or elements of data, some of which have the traditional intellectual property rights, some public domain, and some licensed under different licensing schemes.

Rather than disrupting centuries of foundational work in the protection of intangibles and creating more property rights in 'drops of water' which might gradually find their way to the greater 'oceans of water', the better approach, and the challenge, lies in understanding the many different contexts in which Big Data comes into play. Enabling the legitimate and legal use of Big Data datasets requires the securing of permission from the data custodians or owners of these disparate datasets, perhaps using the model for managing information noted above.

On a practical level, what should be the right balance and level of protection for data held in compilations, datasets and databases, which may have been created at great expense, without impeding the public's access to, and use of, the facts and data for data mining and analysis in the era of Big Data? Getting the right balance is one of our biggest ulti-

---

64 Hemnes, above n 22, 29.
65 White House Big Data Review, above n 4, 28.

mate challenges moving forward.

We are being asked as a society to redefine the balance of private and public interests in data without any clear chart about where Big Data will take us or even how Big Data will work in years to come.

Currently, our legal framework falls short in providing clarity and certainty on the treatment and usage of data products in many areas of commercial endeavour. Law and policy makers, in reviewing and updating intellectual property and other laws, need to be aware of the specific challenges posed by Big Data in the Digital Economy. Legal certainty on the ambit and scope of ownership in Big Data is important to encourage further value and innovation.

With the pervasive use of computer technology, a rapidly growing percentage of our data is created automatically from the use of IoT, sensors, systems collecting transactional data and other devices. As most of the data collected comprises factually-based information, it is unlikely that they would be protected under our traditional intellectual property laws. Should rights be left to the realms of contract, confidential information, trade secrets, unfair competition laws and other mechanisms; or should government provide the custodianship to enhance researchers' access to Big Data?

Some might argue that the best way to encourage and reward creativity is to grant property rights to the creators and the right to control the assets they create. However, with such decentralised control, the cost of assembling the needed datasets for Big Data mining and analysis would be exorbitant, requiring identification of the owners, coordination and interaction with owners of the required datasets.

The deployment of cloud technology and distributed networks are exacerbating the challenges in a rapidly globalised digital economy where data can easily traverse national borders. We need to work with our international counterparts to adopt international standards for the balanced protection of Big Data and its fair use.

Unlike Australia, the EU has its *sui generis* database rights,[66] the UK

---

66 My research indicates that there has been some controversy and debate on the EU databases directive. However, due to word constraints in this essay, I have not ventured down

has additionally implemented specific provisions to protect computer-generated works, and in the US the tort of misappropriation allows owners some control over the use that can be made of their Big Data databases.

The time is ripe to act with some haste and reason in order for us to maximise and to leverage on the benefits of Big Data while minimising its risks and improving our opportunities to foster the growth of our digital economy, innovation and creativity. Big Data is changing our world. Whether this is enough to evolve our laws in relation to the control and ownership of data remains to be seen. Ultimately, the question of whether property analogies are appropriate in the world of Big Data would depend on the nature, context and characteristics of the data itself. 'Big Data has and will continue to shape and change our perspectives of property rights in data.

---

the path to analyse the deficiencies of the current EU databases model. Readers should refer to Estelle Derclaye, *The Legal Protection of Databases: A Comparative Analysis* (Edward Elgar Publishing, 2008) 259 (Ch. 9), which examines the issues in greater detail.

Chapter 3

Taxation of Multinational Enterprises in the Digital Economy

Antony Ting

The digital economy has led to significant changes in business models of multinational enterprises (MNEs). The Organisation for Economic Co-operation and Development (OECD) described the changes in this way:

> All sectors of the economy have adopted [information and communication technology] to enhance productivity, en-large market reach and reduce operational costs … These technologies have also changed the ways in which … products and services are produced and delivered …

The digital economy has also enhanced the ability of MNEs to engage in aggressive tax avoidance structures. Media reports of the 'successful' tax structures of major MNEs such as Apple, Google and Microsoft have put intense pressure on governments to address the issues. However, the international tax regime was developed in the 20th century when the business environment was very different from the digital economy. The challenges arising from the digital economy are significant and require a fundamental reform of the regime.

The aim of this chapter is twofold. First, it analyses a typical tax structure of a MNE engaging in the business of internet advertisement to highlight the challenges imposed by the digital economy on the international tax regime. Second, it reviews and evaluates multilateral and unilateral responses to the challenges to date.

Tax avoidance structures of MNEs in the digital economy

This part briefly analyses a typical tax structure adopted by many digital companies, including Google and Microsoft.[1] Of course, the tax structure of each MNE is different and often evolves over time. Nevertheless, the example serves to highlight the key challenges arising from the digital economy to the current international tax regime.

The tax structure is depicted in the following diagram:

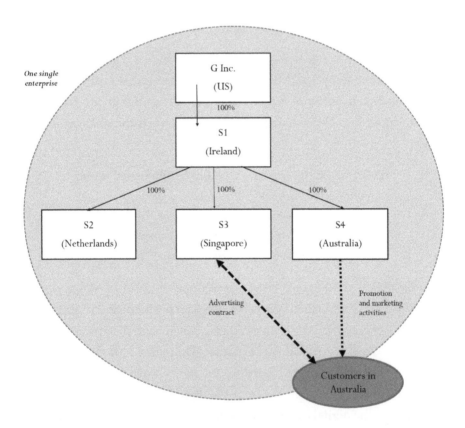

G, the parent company, is incorporated in the US. It provides Inter-

---

1 The tax structure – based on an example in the OECD Base Erosion and Profit Shifting (BEPS) final report on Action 1 – is modified to have a focus on Australia: OECD, *Addressing the Tax Challenges of the Digital Economy, Action 1– Final Report* (2015) ('Action 1 Final Report') 171–5.

net services including search engines to customers worldwide. The R&D activities are virtually all performed by G in the US. However, under a cost-sharing agreement between G and its wholly-owned subsidiary, S1, which is a company incorporated in Ireland with no employees, S1 has the rights to use this technology in non-US markets.

S1 licences the rights in the technology to a wholly-owned sister subsidiary, S2, which is incorporated in the Netherlands and again has no employees. S2 in turn sub-licenses the technology to S3, a company incorporated in Singapore. S3 has employees managing the group's operations in the Asia Pacific region, including Australia. However, it does not have any direct contact with customers in the region. Instead, S4, another wholly-owned subsidiary of S1, is incorporated in Australia and responsible for marketing the advertising business to the customers in the country.

Billions of dollars of advertising income are generated from customers in Australia every year. However, despite no direct contact with customers in Australia, S3 signed the advertising contracts with the Australian customers. The income is therefore booked in Singapore. Most of the income is paid by S3 as royalties to S2, which in turn pays the amount again as royalties to S1. Due to the clever design of the tax structure taking advantage of tax rules in the relevant jurisdictions,[2] the royalties received by S1 are never taxed anywhere in the world.

In Australia, S4 earns a service fee from S3 based on a mark-up of its operating expenses. As a result, minimal profits – as compared to the advertising fees received by S3 in Singapore – are subject to tax in Australia.

The impact of the digital economy is reflected in a couple of features of the structure. First, the intangible assets developed by the group are extremely valuable and therefore justify the significant amount of royalty payments, which effectively shifted profits from source countries such as Australia. Second, the servers that host the websites are located and maintained in different countries around the world. As the OECD explained:[3]

Dependent on the time of the day, different members of the

_____

2 A detailed discussion of these technical tax rules is beyond the scope of this chapter. See OECD, above n 1, for a brief explanation of the relevant rules.
3 OECD above n 1, 172.

group may be responsible for the maintenance of the website
and fixing any network issues in the region.

In practice, it is very difficult to pinpoint the location where the profits are generated in this type of globalised and highly integrated MNE.

These challenges arising from the digital economy are discussed in more detail in the following part.

Challenges to the international tax regime

The existing international tax regime in general adopts the residence and source principles to allocate taxing rights on cross-border transactions between countries. These principles were first developed by the League of Nations in the 1920s.[4] In very broad terms, under the residence principle, if a company is a tax resident of the US (in this case, US is known as the resident country), its worldwide income is subject to US taxation. Under the source principle, if the income of that US company is sourced in Australia (in this case, Australia is known as the source country), Australia also has the taxing right to tax the income. To avoid double taxation, the resident country typically allows the company to claim the Australian tax paid as foreign tax credit in its US tax return.[5]

The concept of permanent establishment

There is inherent tension between residence and source countries as they compete for tax revenue.[6] One of the critical tax policy questions in this international tax competition is how to determine the source for various types of income. This issue is crucial as it determines whether the source

---

4 For a brief discussion of the development of the principles, see OECD, *Addressing Base Erosion and Profit Shifting* (February 2013) 34–5 <http://www.oecd.org/tax/addressing-base-erosion-and-profit-shifting-9789264192744-en.htm>.

5 Foreign tax credit is typically provided under domestic tax law, as well as tax treaties, which reflect the current international consensus on this issue.

6 Richard Vann, 'Current Trends in Balancing Residence and Source Taxation' (Sydney Law School Research Paper No. 14/107, The University of Sydney, December 2014) 1 <http://papers.ssrn.com/sol3/papers.cfm?abstract_id=2538269>. Reform of the current residence and source principles, if it can be achieved at all, would most likely allocate more taxing rights to source countries which are predominantly developing countries: See, for example, Mindy Herzfeld, 'A Looming Global Tax War?' (2016) (81) *Tax Notes International* 467, 468.

42

country has taxing rights on income generated by a company in the country. Under the current international tax norm, which is embedded in over 3,000 bilateral tax treaties, active business income (for example, sales income or service fees) of a foreign company in general is subject to taxation in a source country only if the company has a relatively significant presence in the country, which is known as a permanent establishment (PE).

The concept of PE is critical. If a foreign company has no PE in a country, its active business income in general is not taxable in that country. This is the international consensus achieved in the 20th century. However, this consensus is increasingly being challenged by the digital economy, which facilitates modern MNEs in becoming globally integrated. As the tax structure above shows, it is increasingly common for a MNE in the digital age to design its tax structure to ensure that it does not have a significant presence in a country while generating a significant amount of income from customers in that country. This can happen when the business model of the MNE relies primarily on a digital platform that is intangible in nature and in practice can be 'located' within jurisdictions of its choice, typically low tax countries. As the digital platform is potentially the most valuable and important asset of the business, a significant portion of the MNE's profits could arguably be allocated to the location of the intangible asset.

The OECD describe the issues in this way (emphasis added):[7]

> It had already been recognised way in the past that the concept of permanent establishment referred … to a substantial presence in the country concerned … Nowadays it is possible [for a MNE] to be heavily involved in the economic life of another country, e.g. by doing business with customers located in that country via the internet, without having a taxable presence therein… In an era where non-resident taxpayers can derive substantial profits from transactions with customers located in another country, *questions are being raised as to whether the current rules ensure a fair allocation of taxing rights on business profits*, especially where the profits from such transactions go untaxed anywhere.

7 OECD, above n 4, 35–6.

The separate entity doctrine

As the tax structure above shows, advertising income generated from Australian customers by the corporate group is not taxable in either Australia or the US. This is known as double non-taxation, or stateless income. This tax outcome is possible due largely to the fact that the current international tax regime in general adopts the separate entity doctrine, which dictates that intra-group transactions are respected even if the transactions are created for tax avoidance purposes.[8]

Transfer pricing rules are therefore required to determine the appropriate intra-group pricing. However, as MNEs become highly integrated, a substantial amount of cross-border transactions occur not between independent parties, but within corporate groups. Tax administrations face significant difficulties to determine the transfer pricing for intra-group transactions primarily because comparable transactions between unrelated parties often do not exist.[9]

The position of general respect of intra-group transactions is questionable. From an economic perspective, modern MNEs are so highly integrated that in substance they operate as one single enterprise. It has been argued that to address the challenges imposed by the modern MNEs, the international tax regime requires a paradigm shift and should adopt the enterprise doctrine under which a corporate group under the common control of a parent company should be treated as one single enterprise for tax purposes.[10] This is obviously not a new problem. However, the rapid growth of the digital economy has significantly exacerbated the issue.

The increasing significance of intangible assets

The digitalisation of businesses and the economy also means that intangible assets have become increasingly important and valuable for MNEs.

---

8 General anti-avoidance provisions in the tax laws may apply to tax-driven transactions. However, in practice, the provisions are very difficult to apply to complex structures of MNEs.

9 Vann, above n 6, 4.

10 A detailed discussion of these issues is beyond the scope of this chapter. For a discussion of these issues, see Antony Ting, 'iTax – Apple's International Tax Structure and the Double Non-Taxation Issue' (2014) (1) *British Tax Review* 40, 59–66.

Intangibles present serious problems to the international tax system, as they are inherently mobile. MNEs can locate their intangible assets in a tax haven with relative ease.[11] They are also inherently difficult to value, as they are often developed internally by the MNEs and therefore unique.

The tax structure analysed above is a good example of how MNEs can engage in tax avoidance by manipulation of the unique characteristics of intangible assets. The corporate group under the common control of G has successfully detached the location of the R&D activities that generated the intangible assets from the location where the profits derived from those assets were booked. The profits generated from the intangibles are often booked in low tax countries for tax avoidance purposes.

The problem of taxing intangibles is not new. Back in 1975, several OECD countries already recognised the issues and proposed a radical policy option (emphasis added):[12]

> A more effective approach might be ... not to ... recognise ... the transfer of [intangibles] between related companies in different countries. *It is difficult to see what business purpose is in fact served by such transfers other than tax avoidance ...* Such a solution would go beyond the provisions of a tax convention, but it is not outside the competence of the Committee on Fiscal Affairs to consider.

The development of the digital economy that has gathered pace in recent years has significantly exacerbated the tax issues arising from intangibles.

Responses to the digital economy's challenges to date

The OECD summarises the challenges of the digital economy to the international tax regime in this way:

---

11 There are interesting similarities between the taxation issues of intangibles and shipping income, and lessons may be learnt from the experience of the taxation of shipping income: Vann, above n 6, 9.

12 OECD Working Group No. 21 of Working Party No. 1 (United States, Denmark & Germany), *Draft Report on Tax Avoidance through the Improper Use and Abuse of Tax Conventions*, CFA/WP1(75)3 (21 May 1975) 23 <http://www.taxtreatieshistory.org/>.

The digital economy is characterised by an unparalleled reliance on intangible assets ... and the difficulty of determining the jurisdiction in which value creation occurs. This raises fundamental questions as to ... how the digital economy relates to the concepts of source and residence ... These weaknesses put the existing consensus-based framework at risk, and a bold move by policy makers is necessary to prevent worsening problems.

The following paragraphs analyse multilateral and unilateral responses to the challenges.

Multilateral response – the BEPS Project

The importance of the digital economy in the context of the OECD/G20 base erosion profit shifting (BEPS) project was reflected in the fact that out of the 15 Action Items identified in the project, Action 1 – with the title 'Addressing the Tax Challenges of the Digital Economy' – was devoted to the issue. The critical role of the digital economy played in the BEPS Project has been described in this way:[13]

The BEPS project was born out of the digital economy and the perceived use of 'stateless income' by companies in that economy to avoid tax.

At the commencement of the BEPS project in 2013, the OECD originally set out with an ambitious goal in response to the challenges imposed by the digital economy: to renegotiate the 20th century international consensus on the allocation of taxing rights between residence and source countries. The OECD described the key goal of the project in this way at that stage (emphasis added):[14]

More fundamentally, a holistic approach is necessary to properly address the issue of BEPS. Government actions

13 Greenwoods & Herbert Smith Freehills, *Tax Brief – G20/OECD Deliver BEPS Project But It's Not Over* (9 October 2015) 13 <http://www.greenwoods.com.au/insights/tax-brief/9-october-2015-g20oecd-deliver-beps-project-but-it-s-not-over/>.
14 OECD, above n 4, 50.

should be comprehensive … These include … *the balance between source and residence taxation …*

An example of what this statement might mean is the proposal in France to expand the definition of the PE concept for the digital economy. In particular, a task force on the taxation of the digital economy established by the French government proposed that a PE would be deemed to exist when Internet user data was collected in a domestic market.[15] The proposal was unsurprisingly very controversial and eventually was not adopted by the government. Nevertheless, it demonstrated the general concern about the taxation of digital companies and the possible responses to the challenges of the digital economy on the existing international tax regime.[16]

In a report released by the OECD in July 2013, just a few months after the commencement of the BEPS project, it attempted to calm the nerves of some countries – notably the US – that were strongly opposed to any major change of the international tax regime (emphasis added):[17]

> In the changing international tax environment, a number of countries have expressed a concern about how international standards on which bilateral tax treaties are based allocate taxing rights between source and residence States. While actions to address BEPS will restore both source and residence taxation in a number of cases where cross-border income would otherwise go untaxed or would be taxed at very low rates, *these actions are not directly aimed at changing the existing international standards on the allocation of taxing rights on cross-border income.*

However, in the same report, the OECD reiterated the importance of the digital economy and hinted at the possibility of reform of the source

---

15 Pierre Collin and Nicolas Colin, Task Force on Taxation of the Digital Economy, Report to the Minister for the Economy and Finance, the Minister Delegate for the Budget and the Minister Delegate for Small and Medium-Sized Enterprises, Innovation and the Digital Economy (18 January 2013).

16 Oana Popa, 'Taxation of the Digital Economy in Selected Countries – Early Echoes of BEPS and EU Initiatives' (2015) 55 (1) *European Taxation*, paragraph 2.3.

17 OECD, *Action Plan on Base Erosion and Profit Shifting* ('Action Plan') (July 2013), 11 <http://dx.doi.org/10.1787/9789264202719-en>.

rules in the objective statement for Action 1 'Address the tax challenges of the digital economy' (emphasis added):[18]

> Identify the main difficulties that the digital economy poses for the application of existing international tax rules and develop detailed options to address these difficulties, taking a holistic approach ... Issues to be examined include ... *the ability of a company to have a significant digital presence in the economy of another country without being liable to taxation due to the lack of nexus under current international rules ... the application of related source rules ...*

However, the OECD quickly realised that the goal of reaching a new international consensus on the rules to allocate taxing rights between residence and source countries was too ambitious and unachievable, especially given the tight two-year time frame for the project. In the interim report on Action 1 released by the OECD in September 2014, the original aim of redefining the source rules for the digital economy was not mentioned. Instead, it stated that:[19]

> OECD and G20 countries ... have reached a common understanding of the challenges raised by the digital economy, which will now allow them to deepen their work in this area, one in which BEPS is exacerbated.

At this stage, the OECD seemed to have given up the hope of reaching international consensus for specific tax policy recommendations in Action 1. Instead, the OECD stated that the tax issues arising from the digital economy would be addressed through the work on *other* action items of the BEPS project:[20]

> While the digital economy does not generate unique BEPS issues, some of its key features exacerbate BEPS risks ...

---

18 Ibid 14–15.
19 OECD, *Addressing the Tax Challenges of the Digital Economy – Action 1: 2014 Deliverable* ('Action 1 Interim Report') 4.
20 Ibid 13–14.

These BEPS risks are being addressed in the context of the BEPS Project … Structures aimed at artificially shifting profits to locations where they are taxed at more favourable rates, or not taxed at all, will be addressed by ongoing work in the context of the BEPS Project.

The final report on Action 1 was released by the OECD in October 2015. Specific tax policy recommendations were absent in the report. Instead, it presented 'conclusions regarding the digital economy, the BEPS issues and the broader tax challenges it arises, and *the recommended next steps*' (emphasis added).[21] The recommended next steps were 'to continue working on these issues and to monitor development over time … A report reflecting the outcome of the continued work in relation to the digital economy *should* be produced by 2020' (emphasis added).[22]

In particular, the final report on Action 1 explicitly stated that the Task Force on the digital economy concluded that:[23]

… a new nexus in the form of a significant economic presence … was not recommended at this stage. This is because, among other reasons, it is expected that the measures developed in the BEPS Project will have a substantial impact on BEPS issues previously identified in the digital economy, that certain BEPS measures will mitigate some aspects of the broader tax challenges …

Interestingly, the Report left the option open for countries to unilaterally introduce the option in their domestic tax laws:[24]

Countries could, however, introduce [this option] in their domestic laws as additional safeguards against BEPS, provided they respect existing treaty obligations …

---

21 OECD, Action 1 Final Report, above n 1, 11.
22 Ibid 13.
23 Ibid.
24 Ibid.

Unilateral responses

Before the OECD BEPS project released its final reports, several countries have already taken unilateral actions in response to the pressure of the digital economy imposed on their tax systems. The first country to implement special anti-avoidance measures targeting digital companies is the UK. It introduced the diverted profits tax (DPT) with effect from 1 April 2015.

The DPT is designed to be a separate tax distinct from the corporate income tax. The UK government believes that this design feature will render the tax outside the scope of its tax treaties. The primary policy objective of the DPT is 'to counteract contrived arrangements used by large groups … that result in the erosion of the UK tax base'.[25] In the presentation in a consultation meeting, HM Revenue and Customs (HMRC) stated that the DPT 'also has the secondary aim of removing the information bias to allow for a full and timely examination of high risk transfer pricing transactions by *providing strong incentives for full disclosure* and early engagement in those high risk cases' (emphasis added).[26] This objective is a very important policy driver behind a number of key features of the DPT, which is designed to enhance its deterrent effect on MNEs' zest for tax avoidance.

The legislation of the DPT is complex.[27] In broad terms, the DPT – that imposes a tax of 25 per cent on diverted profits[28] – applies in two situations. First, the tax applies to a UK company involved in an arrangement that creates low-taxed income without sufficient economic substance.[29] Second, the DPT applies to 'foreign companies [that] make substantial

---

25 HM Treasury, Finance (No.2) Bill 2015 – Explanatory Note, Clause 77 paragraph 4.

26 HM Revenue and Customs, *Diverted Profits Tax – Open Day Slides* (February 2015) <https://www.gov.uk/government/publications/diverted-profits-tax-open-day-slides>.

27 For instance, a commentator found the provisions to be 'couched in the mind-numbing legalese that is the specialty of Treasury legal counsel and parliamentary draftsmen. They have exceeded themselves on this occasion …': Sol Picciotto, 'The UK's Diverted Profits Tax: An Admission of Defeat or a Pre-Emptive Strike?' (2015) 77 (3) *Tax Notes International* 239, 239.

28 This rate is 5 per cent higher than the prevailing general corporate tax rate of 20 per cent in the UK.

29 *Finance Act 2015* (UK) c 33, s 80. See also HM Revenue & Customs, *Diverted Profits Tax – Interim Guidance* ('Interim Guidance'), DPT1110.

sales in the UK while avoiding the creation of a UK permanent establishment'.[30] This test is designed to target MNEs with structures similar to
that of Google.[31]

Australia is the second country to introduce a similar unilateral an-
ti-BEPS regime targeting digital companies that attempt to avoid having
a PE in the country. The new regime, known as the Multinational Anti-Avoidance Law (MAAL),[32] is effective from 1 January 2016. It is designed to tackle tax avoidance structures that, in broad terms, are designed
to generate income in Australia but avoid having a PE in the country.

This type of unilateral action aimed at addressing BEPS by MNEs has
been controversial. In particular, countries such as the US have expressed
strong concerns that the unilateral actions were premature and should not
have proceed before the OECD BEPS project delivered the final reports.
However, as discussed above, it seemed obvious, even at the early stage
of the BEPS project, that the project was unlikely to produce effective
anti-avoidance policy recommendations to address some of the key challenges of the digital economy, including the 'avoided PE' tax structures of
Google and Microsoft.

The UK's DPT has already shown some signs of success. Amazon announced in May 2015 that it had started to pay tax on its sales in the UK
rather than in Luxembourg.[33] This came about after Amazon restructured
its tax structure in Europe in response, at least in part, to the DPT. Google
also announced in January 2016 that it had reached a settlement with the
tax authority in the UK to pay £130 million as back taxes and interest covering the 2005–15 tax periods. It will also start paying UK tax on revenue
from UK-based advertisers.[34]

---

30 Interim Guidance, DPT1140.

31 See Example 3, Interim Guidance, at 37–8. This anti-avoidance regime is therefore
commonly known as the Google tax.

32 *Income Tax Assessment Act 1936* (Cth) s 177DA.

33 Simon Bowers, 'Amazon to Begin Paying Corporation Tax on UK Retail Sales', *Guardian* (London), 23 May 2015.

34 The settlement between Google and the UK tax authority has been controversial. The
settlement amount appears to be small compared to the billions of pounds of income
generated from the UK over the period: Stephanie Johnston, 'Google Sparks Controversy
with £130 Million UK Tax Settlement', *Tax Notes* (*Worldwide Tax Daily*), 26 January 2016.
The settlement was subject to a parliamentary enquiry in the UK. For a brief summary of

Conclusion

MNEs have become very aggressive in tax avoidance in recent years. Their ability to do so has been enhanced by the digital economy in several ways. First, the digital economy dictates that intangible assets become more important and valuable for many MNEs. Their mobility and divisibility facilitates the design of tax avoidance structures. Second, the digital economy significantly accelerated the pace of globalisation. MNEs have become so highly integrated that the existing international tax regime struggles to cope with artificial corporate structures and intra-group transactions designed to separate the location of value creation from the location where profits are booked. Third, the digital economy allows MNEs to generate a significant amount of income from a country without any substantial physical presence in that country. This presents a serious challenge to the traditional residence and source principles that are the cornerstones of the international tax regime.

In response to the challenges of the digital economy, the OECD and G20 have embarked on the BEPS project. It aims to achieve an international consensus on policy solutions to address tax avoidance of MNEs. The release of the final reports – which present recommendations to improve various areas in the international tax regime – represents the first phrase of the project. The next phase of the project, namely implementation, will be an even more challenging task. The success of the project will depend largely on how many countries ultimately implement the recommendations, and whether they incorporate any changes to the recommendations.

---

the hearing, see Santhie Goundar, 'Panel Grills Google, HMRC about £130 Million Tax Settlement', *Tax Notes (Worldwide Tax Daily)*, 12 February 2016.

Chapter 4

Internet Finance in China: Digital Disruption and Regulatory Dilemma

Hui (Steven) Feng

To international observers, the world of Chinese finance following the Global Financial Crisis (GFC) has been plagued with worrying issues such as local government debt, banks' exposure to a declining real estate sector and shadow banking. At the same time, however, internet-based financial services have been growing explosively after 2013. Based on the latest Internet technologies, China's private-sector Internet giants are making an aggressive foray into the nation's financial sector and posing serious challenges to the established regulatory framework. This chapter will first examine the rapid development of Internet finance in China in the last three years, how it disrupted the banks' business models and how banks have staged their responses. It will then look at the regulatory dynamics in this area, particularly from the perspective of its main regulator, the People's Bank of China (PBoC), China's central bank. It examines the benefits and risks associated with Internet finance from the regulator's perspective, and how this has led to the establishment of a regulatory regime of Internet finance in China in late 2015.

The Disruption

Internet finance is a loosely used, catch-all term for finance activities and services conducted over the Internet, including online payment, credit, wealth management tools, etc. By moving financial intermediation online,

Internet finance has been able to cut into traditional banking by offering more convenient payment solutions and investment channels with higher returns to consumers and investors.

In China, in particular, there has been a perfect storm of conditions for the meteoric rise of Internet finance. The popularity of mobile handsets in China, thanks to ever-lowering production costs, provide the hardware foundation of Internet services, especially e-commerce and the associated online payment systems. Under a regime of financial repression, online wealth management products (WMPs) generate returns twice as high as traditional banks for the emerging middle-class with increasing liquidity, whilst online credits channel funds to individual borrowers and small businesses that have been kept out of the formal realm of finance.

There have been three main components of the booming industry of Internet finance in China: online payment platforms, WMPs and online credits (peer-to-peer lending, or P2P).

Online Payment Platforms

Internet finance in China largely originated from digital payment systems, which has in turn benefited from the rise of e-commerce as a result of rising household disposable incomes. For example, Alibaba, China's largest e-commerce company, recorded a whopping $14.3 billion sales during its Singles Day promotion, China's version of the Cyber Monday.[1] Accordingly, by January 2016, Alibaba has over 400 million registered Chinese users on its online payment platform, Alipay, as well as 270 million monthly active users of Alipay Wallet, the mobile version of the Alipay based on quick response (QR) codes.[2] Compare that to Paypal, a major international player in this business, which only has 169 million.[3]

---

1 Bloomberg Technology, 'Alibaba Singles' Day Sales Reach $14.3 Billion, Smashing Record', *Bloomberg News* (online), 10 November 2015 <http://www.bloomberg.com/news/articles/2015-11-10/why-alibaba-is-having-singles-day-in-beijing-for-first-time>.
2 Craig Smith, 'By the Numbers: 22 Crazy Alipay Statistics' on *Digital Marketing Ramblings* (DMR) (1 April 2016) <http://expandedramblings.com/index.php/alipay-statistics/>.
3 Lincoln E Davidson, 'The Bumpy Road to Regulating China's Internet Finance Industry', *The Diplomat*, 5 August 2015.

These third-party digital platforms offer online shoppers the chance to accumulate reward points, while consumers are able to top-up their accounts through smartphones and at convenience stores. They have also been developing offline payment capabilities for face-to-face transactions. Chinese consumers made RMB 9.5 trillion in mobile payments through third-party service providers in 2015, up from RMB 6 trillion and RMB 1.2 trillion in 2014 and 2013 respectively, according to iResearch estimates (see Figure 1).

Figure 1. Online and mobile payments in China, 2009–15

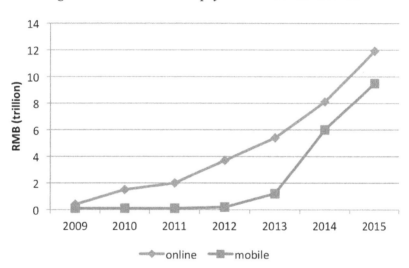

Source: iResearch (2016) 2015 China Internet Finance Summary Report.

While in many other markets the bulk of online transactions are paid for by credit or debit cards, third-party payment systems predominate in China, meaning that Internet companies are cutting out the traditional financial sector.

The emergence of third-party online payments is hurting the banks' bottom lines. In a traditional credit card transaction, the merchant pays a 1–2 per cent fee that is split between the banks and the payment processor (usually China Unionpay). The banks generally receive over half of this amount. With a transaction on a third-party platform, however, banks get only a fraction of the fees received through traditional payment means.[4]

Online Wealth Management

WMPs provided on the Internet are essentially money market funds (MMFs) that collect retail investments into interbank markets through negotiated deposits, accounting for more than 60 per cent of Internet MMF assets. These also transform Internet companies into some of China's largest fund managers. For example, Alibaba's Yu'ebao is the most popular online WMP; an instant success that attracted 124 million buyers in the year after its June 2013 launch. By the end of 2015, Yu'ebao had over 260 million users and assets worth RMB 627 billion.[5] This turned Tianhong, the asset management firm that manages the product (in which Alibaba owns a majority stake), into China's largest mutual fund by assets.[6]

The online WMPs have been extremely popular in China for several reasons. First, online WMPs offer comparatively high annual yields by making demand deposit accounts paid at de facto market interest rates that Chinese consumers cannot get from banks. By lowering the minimum investment of publicly offered funds from 1,000 yuan to only one yuan, these online WMPs have made MMFs more accessible to the masses, particularly the younger generations who are the most active users of the internet in China.[7] Last but not least, these online WMPs are attractive because they are extremely liquid. They can generally be redeemed on the same day compared with two to three days by traditional MMFs, and a few weeks by those issued by banks.[8]

---

4 PriceWaterhouseCoopers (PwC), *Banking and Finance in China: The Outlook for 2015* (January 2015) <http://www.pwccn.com/webmedia/doc/635585738589999909_bfic_2015.pdf>.
5 'Yu'ebao users exceed 260 million', *Shenzheng tequ bao*, 27 January 2016.
6 Ibid.
7 Takeshi Jingu, 'Internet Finance Growing Rapidly in China' (10 March 2014) 189 *Iakyara*.
8 PwC, above n 4.

As a result, China's state-controlled banks have been losing market share of the nation's 48 trillion yuan in household savings. For example, the four largest firms controlled 50.8 per cent of the country's yuan-denominated household savings as of 31 Jan. 2014, down from 52 per cent a year earlier and 55 per cent in 2012 (see also Figure 2).[9]

Figure 2. Exodus of retail deposits from banks

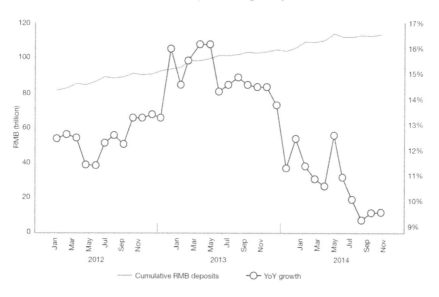

Source: PwC (2015).

P2P Lending

While online WMPs attract more risk-averse, conservative investors, web-based P2P lending appeals to a smaller group of wealthier investors who cut-out banks and lend directly to each other over online platforms. P2P lending totalled an estimated over RMB 830 billion in 2015, up from RMB 68 billion in 2013 (see Figure 3).

---

9 Bloomberg Technology, 'China Banks Drained by 'Vampire' Internet Funds', *Bloomberg News* (online), 25 March 2014 <http://www.bloomberg.com/news/articles/2014-03-24/china-banks-drained-by-funds-called-vampires-seek-rules>.

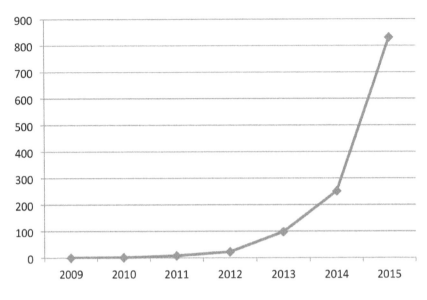

Figure 3. P2P lending in China, 2009–15

Source: PwC (2015); iResearch (2016).

Coping Strategies of the Establishment

To be sure, the rapid growth of Internet finance in China has been propelled not by the established financial institutions (banks), but non-financial companies, most notably e-commerce and other Internet companies. As discussed above, conducting (financial) businesses online has caused disruption to the traditional banks by providing a more convenient platform for payment and a more lucrative alternative for savings and investment.

After the initial 'shock-and-awe', the banking and financial sector hit back with a combination of strategies. The initial strategy has been defensive as a knee-jerk reaction to the challenge. Internet funds, such as Yu'ebao, were accused of being 'a vampire sucking blood out of the banks and a typical financial parasite' that 'didn't create value'.[10] Verbal allegations were accompanied by actions. At least three of China's biggest banks have refused to take negotiable deposits from Yu'e Bao. Some banks have also set limits on their customers' transfers to services such as Yu'ebao and

10 Ibid.

Licaitong (an online WMP issued by Tencent). For example, China Merchant bank and Minsheng Bank limit transfers to Licaitong accounts to RMB 5,000 per day.[11] At the same time, the banks had called for the regulators to curb its rapid expansion, demanding a level playing field with Internet companies alleged to have benefited from the absence of regulation for capital, liquidity and provision requirements. In particular, the banks have ignited a nationwide debate on whether online funds should be subject to a reserve requirement: a regulatory institution that sets the minimum fraction of customer deposits and notes that a commercial bank must park in the central bank as reserves (rather than lend out). They argue that the investment collected by online WMPs are essentially deposits, thus the online MMFs should also be subject to the same capital restraints as the banks. According to an estimate by a PBoC official, the annualised return of Yu'e Bao would be reduced by one percentage point if there were a 20 per cent reserve requirement on the portion of the Internet fund's money placed as deposits with banks.[12] Eventually the PBoC gave in to the banks' demands and ruled that the deposits by financial institutions (including online funds) at the banks would be subject to reserve requirement from the beginning of 2015, but the ratio has been kept at zero. This nonetheless opened the door for restrictions on the online WMPs in the future.

With the rapid growth of the online sector, China's banks came to realise that they could not nip the online business in the bud, and that they must adapt to the new world of the Internet. In other words, China's banks must respond with a real competitive offering to consumers; rather than relying on the central bank to grant them a competitive advantage through restrictive rules on their competitors. Hence, the banking sector adopted a bandwagon strategy by setting up 'direct banks', which offer services over the Internet or telephone instead of through branches. In 2014, for instance, as many as 15 banks launched web-based direct banking for wealth management, credit card repayments and other services.[13]

11 PwC, above n 4, 39.
12 'PBOC Official: Banks Should Hold Reserves on Yu'ebao Deposits', *Wall Street Journal* (online), 5 May 2015 <http://www.wsj.com/articles/SB10001424052702303417104579542951778332662>.
13 PwC, above n 4, 38.

There have been two different approaches for banks going directly online. China Minsheng Bank, on the one hand, aims to become a completely independent direct bank, and has adopted a purely online model, with a strategic goal of servicing long-tail markets such as low-end retail customers and micro and small enterprises. The Bank of Beijing, on the other hand, has borrowed the experiences of ING Direct by adopting an online and offline model, with a core strategic goal of attracting deposits at low costs.[14] There is great potential for direct banking in China, given the increasingly extensive penetration of Internet and mobile banking. According to a survey from Accenture, more than 21 per cent of Chinese customers have completely switched to direct banking with potential for further growth, as more than 60 per cent of the Chinese population look to shift more to direct banking methods (see also Figure 4).[15]

Figure 4. Market Size of Direct Banks in China

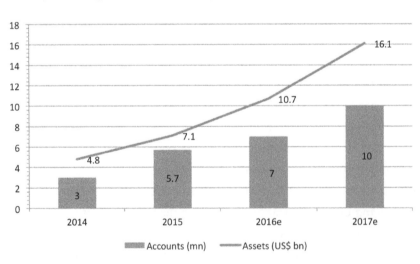

Source: Almanac of China's Finance and Banking 2014,
National Bureau of Statistics, China; Zhang (2015).

14 Hua Zhang, 'China's Direct Banks: Birth of a New Banking Sector', *Celent* (online), 5 January 2015 <http://www.celent.com/reports/chinas-direct-banks-birth-new-banking-sector>.
15 Baron Laudermilk, 'Chinese Banks Enhancing Direct Banking Channels to Cater to Increased Demand', *The Asian Banker* (online), 22 May 2013 <http://www.theasianbanker.com/research-notes/chinese-banks-enhancing-direct-banking-channels-to-cater-to-increased-demand>.

The third strategy of the banks in competing against Internet companies in China has been that of divide-and-rule, which involves either teaming up with external partners or cooperating with the Big Three. A good example of the first approach has been the introduction of Apple Pay by the China UnionPay (CUP) in February 2016. The CUP is essentially a state-backed payment monopoly based on an association of domestic banks. As discussed earlier, the online third-party payment platforms, such as Alipay, have been cutting deeply into the banks' margins in the payment industry, particularly in the mobile payment market, with a share of almost 70 per cent. The partnership between the CUP and Apple will help the latter crack open the potentially largest mobile market in the world. Apple has 19 of China's biggest lenders as partners, which means 80 per cent of China's credit and debit cards are eligible for Apple Pay, usable at about one-third of all locations that accept those cards.[16] For the CUP, this is also a good deal. Apple charges Chinese banks only 0.07 per cent of each transaction compared with the 0.15 per cent it charges banks in the United States.[17] This will increase the banks' margin in handling payments, and will help them defend the market that they are losing to Alibaba and Tencent, hence redraw the strategic landscape in this market segment.

At the same time, the banks also sought to play into the competitive game between the three Internet giants in China. In recent years, China's Internet world has been increasingly dominated by three internet companies, Baidu, Alibaba, and Tencent (collectively known as BAT). While each holds commanding market shares in their core business (Baidu in search engines, Alibaba in e-commerce and Tencent in social networks), BAT has been branching into other business areas, particularly Internet finance. As Table 1 suggests, BAT has become a dominant player in virtually all sub-sections of the Internet finance market.

---

16 Paul Carsten, 'Apple Pay Takes On China's Internet Kings in Mobile Payments', *Reuters* (online), 18 February 2016 <http://www.reuters.com/article/us-apple-payment-china-idUSKCN0VQ302>.

17 Zhang Yuzhe, 'Chinese Banks to Pay Much Smaller Fees to Apple Pay than US Counterparts', *Caixin* (online), 22 February 2016 <http://english.caixin.com/2016-02-22/100911334.html>.

Table 1. The BAT and Internet Finance in China

	Alibaba	Tencent	Baidu
Payment	Alipay	Wechat Wallet	Baidu Wallet
Wealth Management	Yu'ebao	Licaitong	Products and services in cooperation with major banks
P2P/micro-lending	Ant Financial; Ali Microfinance	Funds managed through WeChat	
Direct Banking	MyBank	WeBank	Baixin Bank (with CITIC)

Source: author's data collection.

Among BAT, Baidu has been a relative latecomer in the online financial market compared with Alibaba and Tencent, and it has been eager to penetrate this strategic sector. The banks have seized this opportunity and sought to forge business partnerships with Baidu in various areas in playing the catch-up game. For example, China's largest bank, the Industrial and Commercial Bank of China (ICBC) has teamed-up with Baidu in a strategic partnership in June 2015, which will enable both sides to cooperate in areas such as Internet finance, map service, online marketing, business financing and life services. China's CITIC bank and Baidu also set-up a direct bank in November 2015, dubbed Baixin Bank, in which CITIC takes a controlling stake. The latest partnership would combine CITIC's financial products with Baidu's massive online traffic data, which is expected to present a more credible challenge to the MyBank and We-Bank run by Alibaba and Tencent respectively.

In summary, the traditional banking sector's response to the rise of Internet finance has evolved from early defensive reactions to a more proactive approach. This industry is still at the technology-driven stage, which gives the Internet companies an edge in competing against the banks. However, as the banks ramp-up the pace of adaptation, the online finance sector started drawing concerns from the regulatory authorities.

The Regulatory Dilemma

The rapid rise of Internet finance has not only caused disruption to the industry, but also presents challenges for regulators. For the Chinese government, Internet finance is a relationship of love and hate. While online banking will be one of the critical sectors in facilitating China's industrial upgrade and economic transition, it could also cause financial and social instability without proper regulation. This sets the tone for the relevant policies of the PBoC, which is the major authority in regulating the sector. This has led to policy dilemmas on the part of the central bank, which has been the champion of financial liberalisation in China but also an anchor for financial stability. In addition, the turf wars between PBoC and the related bureaucratic institutions have also made the regulation of Internet finance in China more complicated and dynamic.

Internet Finance That is in Need

To the Chinese authorities, Internet finance emerged at the right time when China was planning to boost a decelerating economy through advanced digitalisation. The Chinese economy had slowed down from a double-digit growth rate in the 1990s and 2000s to a more modest 7 per cent since 2014. The GFC has hit the Western world (traditional buyers of Chinese exports) hard; increases in real wages has been hurting industry margins; and, public investment has also ceased to be an engine of the economy in an efficient way. These factors mean that China needs to change its growth model, traditionally reliant on state-led investment and manufacturing geared toward external demand, to one that is more centred on service and consumption. One critical path to achieving this is industrial upgrade, which for China is to climb the value chain from the low-end to a higher level through research and innovation utilising the Internet revolution.

Hence, on 5 March 2015, Premier Li Keqiang unveiled the national strategy of Internet Plus, which has identified the development of Internet services as an important way to boost industrial innovation and catch-up with advanced economies. In particular, it aims 'to integrate mobile Internet, cloud computing, big data, and the Internet of Things with modern manufacturing, to encourage the healthy development of e-commerce, industrial networks, and Internet banking, and to get Internet-based companies to increase their presence in the international market'.[18] Internet

---

18 'China Unveils Internet Plus Action Plan to Fuel Growth', The State Council, People's

finance occupies a unique position in the Internet Plus strategy. The web-based finance industry has been benefiting from the advancement of Internet technologies. It has, in turn, fuelled a wave of innovation, entrepreneurship and developments in the service sector in China that has helped mitigate the general slowdown of the Chinese economy.

Internet financing also serves as an important vehicle for the central bank's agenda in liberalising the banking and financial sector. China's banking system has been dominated by state-owned banks whose major income relies on an almost guaranteed margin in borrowing and lending thanks to the interest rate regulations of the State. However, cheap funding costs have enabled banks to fuel industry overcapacity and excessive borrowing by state-owned enterprises and local governments, leading to low efficiency in the allocation of financial resources. The PBoC, under the leadership of its governor Zhou Xiaochuan, has been pushing for unprecedented changes in the banking system, including deposit insurance and deregulating interest rates, and to give markets a bigger role in the economy.[19]

Internet finance fits right into the Bank's problem-solving strategy by contributing to its market-driven financial deregulation. The online products can be likened to US financial innovations in the early 1980s in that they have made demand deposit accounts that pay de facto market interest rates available to Chinese consumers. As Ma Weihua, a former president of China Merchants Bank admitted candidly, 'Why is all the money going into Yu'E Bao? Because banks fail to pay what savers deserve. You can't fool them … Yu'E Bao is forcing banks to face up to the challenges of interest-rate deregulation'.[20]

At the same time, the online credit sector can also help channel funds to individuals and particularly small and medium enterprises that, for a long time, have been disadvantaged in the formal banking system, which favours large State firms. During his visit to the WeBank, an online bank by Tencent, Chinese Premier Li said that Internet banking 'will lower

Republic of China, updated 4 July 2015 <http://english.gov.cn/policies/latest_releases/2015/07/04/content_281475140165588.htm>.

19 Stephen Bell and Hui Feng, *The Rise of the People's Bank of China: The Politics of Institutional Change* (Harvard University Press, 2013).

20 Bloomberg Technology, above n 9.

costs for and deliver practical benefits to small clients, while forcing traditional financial institutions to accelerate reforms'.[21] Together with shadow banking, the pairing of the Internet and financial services is driving market-based financial innovation in areas such as interest rate liberalisation, liberalisation of business models, and cross-sectoral market entry.

Risks to Stability

The Chinese government, especially the central bank, has been taking a more tolerant if not supportive role in online banking, but with the rapid growth of the new industry, risks have emerged and caused concern to the regulator and the public.

For instance, risks have emerged in the online WMP market. Some online fund products launched after Yu'ebao's success were offering rates of return well above the market rate, which were seen as a concern. This was because these fund sponsors were not only providing a fund sales platform, but also boosting their funds' apparent rates of return by paying bonus interest funded from sources other than their funds' investment returns without adequate risk disclosure. Some of them are alleged to have engaged in unlawful fund sales.[22]

So far the major risks have been in the P2P lending area where ordinary consumers cut banks out and lend directly to each other over online platforms. The combined factors of low interest rates on savings accounts, a cooling housing market and a volatile stock market, have left many looking for alternatives to park their cash. Web-based micro credits through P2P platforms thus became a convenient channel for retail investors with almost 3,500 P2P platforms across the country by the end of November 2015 (by comparison, there are less than 200 such firms in the US), of which 46 per cent are assessed as 'problematic'.[23] An absence of regulation in this area (with no entry barrier) has led to shady practices and mismanagement, particularly at the lower end of the market. According to a research report by

---

21 PwC, above n 4, 38.

22 Jingu, above n 7.

23 'Jinbanshu P2P Wei Zhengchang Yunzhuan, Qicheng Wenti Pingtai Xuanze Paolu' ('Nearly Half of the P2P Platforms Not in Normal Operation with 70 Per Cent Problematic Ones Shuttered'), *Caixin*, 9 December 2015.

Morgan Stanley, more than 370 peer-to-peer lenders have already closed since China's first P2P lending website launched in 2007. Coupled with a slowing economy and tightening monetary policy, on average, there were 9.3 new platforms at risk of failing every month in the first half of 2014, rising to 92 by the end of 2014, mostly due to fraud and cash flow difficulties, with many instances in which operators fled with their clients' money.[24]

As a result, the P2P area became the online equivalent of the Wild West. It became worse in 2015 as P2P platforms that were supposed to funnel micro loans to small businesses instead featured investment products channelling money into risky areas, such as real estate and stock market. In particular, part of the P2P industry became a platform for investors using borrowed money to trade stocks, which had helped fuel a surge in Chinese stock markets that saw the Shanghai Composite Index rise 150 per cent over twelve months up until June 2015. The subsequent tumble in the stock market wiped some US $3 trillion off China's stock market. The malpractice in the P2P industry ultimately developed into the Ezubao scandal erupting in February 2016, in which almost one million investors lost US $7.6 billion from the P2P lender's Ponzi scheme.[25]

A Regulatory Regime for Internet Finance

The spike in online investor fraud raised concerns on the part of the PBoC as segments of the fast-growing Internet business, without proper regulation, are increasingly jeopardising financial (and further, social) stability. The crash in the stock market in June 2015 led to enormous pressure on the Chinese Premier Li Keqiang, who prompted the central bank to head off any more financial calamities in the wake of the stock market blow-up. This marked the end of the PBoC's largely hands-off approach towards Internet finance.

On 18 July 2015, together with the other nine ministries, the PBoC

---

24 'Shelly Banjo, 'Nearly A Quarter of Chinese Peer-to-Peer Lenders Have Already Failed', *Quartz* (online), 4 June 2015 <http://qz.com/419494/nearly-a-quarter-of-chinese-peer-to-peer-lenders-have-already-failed>.
25 Emily Rauhala, 'How A Huge Chinese 'Ponzi Scheme' Lured Investors', *Washington Post* (online), 8 February 2016 <https://www.washingtonpost.com/world/asia_pacific/how-a-huge-chinese-ponzi-scheme-lured-investors/2016/02/08/fcbae776-ca9c-11e5-b9ab-26591104bb19_story.html>.

issued its first major regulatory package titled the 'Guiding Opinions on Promoting the Healthy Development of Internet Finance'.[26] It clarifies regulatory responsibilities among government departments. The PBoC will supervise online payments, while the China Banking Regulatory Commission, the banking watchdog, will be in charge of regulating Internet loans (including P2P), trust funds and consumer finance; equity-based crowd-funding comes under the China Securities Regulatory Commission, and online insurance sales regulation will be handled by the China Insurance Regulatory Commission.

On an upbeat note, the regulatory Guideline recognises the positive role of Internet finance for the Chinese economy. It called for broadening channels of financing and supporting private investment funds to back the Internet finance industry, including allowing high-performing and qualified Internet finance firms to list. Tax breaks are also recommended for qualifying small enterprises, including start-ups.

However, the main business of the directive is the regulation of Internet finance. The Guideline, together with another set of draft rules released on 31 July 2015, introduces China's first regulatory regime for Internet finance with a series of regulatory principles, including:

- Establishing an online third party depository and custodian system for customers' funds;
- Establishing information disclosure, risk disclosure and qualified investor systems;
- Protecting consumer rights and interests;
- Strengthening network and information security;
- Fulfilling anti-money laundering obligations and preventing Internet financial crimes;
- Strengthening self-regulation and planning to establish the Association of China Internet Financial Industry;

---

26 The other nine Chinese authorities are the Ministry of Industry and Information Technology, the Ministry of Public Security, the Ministry of Finance, the State Administration for Industry and Commerce, The Legislative Affairs Office, the China Banking Regulatory Commission, the China Securities Regulatory Commission, the China Insurance Regulatory Commission and the State Internet Information Office.

- Statistical monitoring and information sharing mechanisms, and
- Reinforcing the regulation of the Ministry of Industry and Information Technology on websites and of State Internet Information Office on the content of websites.

Conclusion

The emergence and fast-growth of Internet finance has presented serious challenges to traditional brick-and-mortar banks by disrupting the latters' business model, which has been based on cheap deposit and a guaranteed margins in lending (around 3 per cent). But more importantly, Internet finance has also disrupted the business model of the Chinese State by empowering household savers and small businesses instead of channelling funds to the State-owned enterprises. Although it also serves the need of facilitating innovation and competition, the disruptions it brings to the State's financial regime of directed credit and the risks to financial and social stability due to its rapid development, mean that the regulation of the sector is necessary and imminent, but also sensitive and dynamic. On the one hand, regulation must catch-up with technological development of the industry. More profoundly, however, the challenge will be for the Chinese authorities to exploit the opportunities of digital disruption to establish a fair, transparent, and competitive market that serves the greater purpose of economic transition based on consumption and innovation.

Chapter 5

Digital Finance in China: The Internet Era

Eva Huang and Louie Bai

In a person's daily life in the 21ˢᵗ century, e-commerce has become a very common term. The general image conjured up by E-commerce is that of online businesses providing goods or agency services on an online platform.

In the western world, the term e-commerce is usually linked to an online seller, such as eBay[1] and Amazon.[2] The development of Internet technology (and other relevant factors such as security, password management and recognition of users' identification), online sale of goods and services is not the only type of business activities that can be facilitated by the Internet. This chapter is an overview of China's digital finance market as an example of these new business activities. It presents how the market has developed, and its potential impact on traditional financial operators. Traditional banks are competitors of these new online financial operators,[3] this chapter also reviews how traditional banks have reacted to the new market situation.

The development of China's digital finance was caused by the demand for online payment systems to facilitate online goods and services transac-

---

1 eBay (2 Apr 2016) < http://www.ebay.com.au/>.

2 Amazon (2 Apr 2016) < https://www.amazon.com/gp/css/homepage.html/ref=ya_surl_youracct>.

3 李学仁, 熊争艳 [Xueren LI and Zhengyan XIONG], 《建行行长声称银行是弱势群体引李克强大笑》'CEO of China Construction Bank (CCB) claimed that banks are the "vulnerable group", which made Primer Li Keqiang's laugh', *Xinhua News Agency*, 4 March 2015.

tions. As the number of transactions continue to grow, digital financial service providers allow their users to deposit money in their online-platform accounts such as a 'wallet', as a result, providers of digital financial services keep a large amount of cash in the online payment system transaction accounts of users, the funds are then available to be pooled and invested in short-term money markets. Online based service providers found that it is possible for them to use such funds in the same way as banks and other financial institutions would, so they started to pay interest that is higher than the savings account interest paid by banks to their users, who deposit money in their online payment system accounts. The online payment systems are directly linked to the platform's business. Due to the incentives provided by interest payments, users are attracted to deposit more money and these operators began to offer loans and provide other financial products. At this point, e-commerce platforms that engaged in these financial activities began to act as a financial services providers.

Online finance in China has gone through a rapid development process. According to the *China Internet Crowd Funding 2014 Annual Report*,[4] crowd funding, an important part of online finance, raised more than RMB 900 million in 2014. By the end of September 2015, the loan balance of the P2P sector had increased to RMB 317.64 billion. Online finance leader Zhejiang Ant Small & Micro Financial Services Group Co., Ltd., a related entity to Alibaba Group, issued unsecured loans of more than RMB 3,000 billion to Taobao merchants.

Online finance has been appealing because of its high yield, low entry barrier and low document requirements.[5] For example, the 7-day annualised yield offered by Yu'E Bao, a money market fund[6] account from Ant

4 China Impact Fund, *China Crowdfunding Report* (October 2014) <http://www.ied.cn/ sites/default/files/CIF%20China%20Crowdfunding%20Report_Final.pdf>.
5 Bryan Zhang, Luke Deer, Robert Wardrop, Andrew Grant, Kieran Garvey, Susan Thorp, Tania Ziegler, Ying Kong, Xinwei Zheng, Eva Huang, Hongyi Chen, John Burton, Duoqi Xu, Gui Chen, Alexis Lui, Ziyuan Bai & Yvonne Gray, *Harnessing Potential the Asia – Pacific Alternative Finance Benchmarking Report, Cambridge Centre for Alternative Finance*, University of Cambridge Judge Business School, Tsinghua University, & The University of Sydney Business School (March 2016, Published in Chinese).
6 U.S. Securities and Exchange Commission, *Money Market Funds* <http://www.sec.gov/ spotlight/money-market.shtml> (2 Apr 2016).

Financials, was 2.83%. However, the average of the concurrent interest rate provided by banks was only 0.35%, and 1-year interest rate was around 2.00%. Access to traditional financial instruments require an individual to have at least RMB 50,000 in savings.

China's mobile payment market is sizable. According to the *Chinese Third-Party Mobile Payment Market Quarterly Monitoring Report 2Q 2015*[7] released by Analysis International, China's third-party mobile payment market transactions reached RMB 3.47 trillion, with accumulated growth of 22.81%. Alipay continues to occupy the leadership position with 74.31% market share.

The following section introduces China's key players in the digital financial market, and discusses their financial services activities. Finally, this chapter will also give a brief discussion of the impact of these new market players on the traditional banking sector, and discusses the differences between traditional banks' services and digital financial operators.

Key Players of China's Digital Finance Market

This section introduces the key players in the digital finance market whose financial services were developed from an e-commerce platform. The characteristics of the services provided by these e-commerce based financial service providers are different. The key players are JD[8], Tencent[9] and Alibaba.[10] JD and Tencent are collectively called the Tencent Camp.[11]

1. Tencent[12]

Tencent, established in 1998, is currently the largest online services provider with the largest number of users in China. Tencent provides many

---

7 Analysys, *Chinese Third-Party Mobile Payment Market Quarterly Monitoring Report 2Q 2015* (3 Mar 2016). <http://www.analysys.cn/yjgd/12237.shtml>.

8 JD (2 Apr 2016) < http://www.jd.com/>.

9 Tencent (2 Apr 2016) <http://www.qq.com/>.

10 Alibaba (2 Apr 2016) <https://www.1688.com/>.

11 163 Technological News, 《腾讯入股京东收购京东上市前15%股份》 [Tencent merges JD 15% of ordinary share before JD's IPO] (10 March 2014) <http://tech.163.com/14/0310/08/9MVAOH1K000915BF.html>.

12 Tencent, Inc, *History of Tencent* (3 Mar 2016) <http://www.tencent.com/en-us/index.shtml>.

types of services such as online communication tools (Wechat[13] and QQ[14]), online gaming, web portals, a movie platform, and software and mobile phone apps. Tencent was listed in Hong Kong Stock Exchange from 2004 and it is recognised as the most successful online-based services business in China.

Previously, Tencent introduced 'Q coin' as a wallet function for users to buy Q coins, but it was not very successful, because Tencent did not develop a satisfactory network for the physical sale of goods. Tencent used to have an online goods selling platform similar to Alibaba and JD, but neither the Q coin payment system[15] nor the platform was a success; Tencent had not developed their payment and financial services system as what Alibaba did.

In order to compete with its main competitor Alibaba, in both goods selling and the financial market, in 2014 Tencent acquired through direct and indirect means approximately 20%[16] of JD shares, with an option to increase its shareholding, and merge its online selling business with JD, which has one of the leading systems of financial services, including payment by instalment, debt issuing and Crowd funding. The combined Tencent Camp (the combination of Tencent and JD[17]) became a significant online services provider and sales of digital finance and goods.

2. JD[18]

JD (or JD.com) is the largest 'self-selling' e-commercial services provider in China. Self-selling means the platform provider also sells goods in its

---

13 Tencent Technology Shenzhen Company Limited, *WeChat App*, 21 Mar 2016.

14 Tencent QQ (2 Apr 2016) <http://im.qq.com/pcqq/>.

15 Q coins pre-pay (2 Apr 2016) <http://pay.qq.com/ipay/index.shtml?c=qqacct_save&ch=qqcard,kj,weixin&n=60&aid=pay.index.header.paycenter&ADTAG=pay.index.header.paycenter>.

16 徐国允Guoyun XU, 《京东腾讯交易详解: 腾讯或成第一大股东》[Details on Tencent and JD's acquisition: Tencent might become the largest shareholder] (11 March 2014) <http://tech.163.com/14/0311/08/9N1RJE3O0000915BF.html>.

17 163 Technological News, 《腾讯入股京东收购京东上市前15%股份》 [*Tencent merges JD 15% of ordinary share before JD's IPO*], 10 March 2014, <http://tech.163.com/14/0310/08/9MVAOH1K000915BF.html>.

18 JD.com, 《关于京东》 [*About JD*] (2 Apr 2016) <http://www.jd.com/intro/about.aspx>.

own inventory. Although its major business is still online selling, the major difference is that its focus point is not on providing a platform for other sellers but purchasing and selling on its own inventory. JD only provides a small proportion of goods that are sold by other sellers.

JD was established in 1998 as a wholesaler of computer accessories. 2004 was the year it introduced its e-commerce website, and became quite successful in the next 10 years. In 2013, JD began establishing its 'financial group' and the Vice-CEO Wei Fan announced that JD would provide small value debt, secured loans, invoice trading and various types of financial services.[19] In 2014, Tencent acquired 20% of its shares. As a result JD, as a part of the Tencent Camp, combined its resources with Tencent in order to compete with its main competitor, Alibaba.

3. *Alibaba*[20]

Alibaba was established in Hangzhou China in 1999. In the early days of the Alibaba group, the company used to operate as an online clothing wholesaler.[21] In 2003, Alibaba established its first online retail platform 'Taobao', which is famous for providing platforms for different types of sellers to sell their goods and services. In December 2004, Alibaba introduced its online payment tool Alipay.[22] In 2005, Alibaba acquired Yahoo! China, and in 2007, Alibaba Limited (a subsidiary of Ali Group) was listed on the Hong Kong Stock Exchange. In 2014, Alibaba's founder Ma Yun (Jack Ma) established Ant Financial, and it took over most of the financial services business and subsidiaries of Alibaba Group. It became a separate group in the same year Alibaba was listed on the NASDAQ in New York. On 10 February 2015, Ant Financial completely took over all financial subsidiaries (including Alipay) of Alibaba Group. Since this point, the Alibaba Group and Ant Financial (which is widely recognised

---

19 陈相明 [Xiangming CHEN], 《京东杀入P2P网贷,》 [JD enters the P2P Online Debts Market], *Shenzhen Business*, 27 August 2013 <http://szsb.sznews.com/html/2013-08/27/content_2601182.htm>.
20 Alibaba Group, *The History of Alibaba* (2 Apr 2016) <http://www.alibabagroup.com/cn/about/history>.
21 Ibid.
22 Which refers to Chinese '支付宝'.

as Alibaba's financial segment) legally became two separate groups. The entity listed on NASDAQ is the non-financial arm of what is colloquially known as the 'Alibaba Group', while the financial segment is held by Ma Yun (Chair and founder of Alibaba) and other institutional holders. According to the CEO of Ant Financial, Peng Lei, Ant Financial is an important co-operator and supplier (of payment services) to Alibaba, but Alibaba and Ant financial are independent legal entities not affiliated with each other.[23] Unlike Tencent, Alibaba's development in the financial sector is the result of their successful online sales of goods and services, while Tencent is a pure services provider.

The next section explains eight types of financial services these online services providers offer. Since there are a large number of different online services providers, it is not possible to include all the players in the sector. This section only explains the players that are representative or are market leaders in some form.

Services Available in the Online Financial Sector

This section categorises eight types of online services that are financial in nature. These services are collectively defined as 'E-Finance Services'. These eight types of E-Finance Services are: payment system, wallet with payment function, instalments, borrowing and lending, money market fund, consumer finance, crowd funding and financing agency services. E-Finance Services are derivatives of e-commerce platforms as they originated from facilitating the payments for online purchases.

1. Direct Payment System

The most common and basic type of service is the direct online payment system. At the beginning of the development of the E-Finance market, it was the first type of service available for online buyers. The service provided is very simple: the payer enters their bank account information on the payment system and the target payee's information; for a services fee the system then uses the given information (such as the payer's purchase

---

23 谢璞 [Pu XIE], 《一张图读懂蚂蚁金服,》 [*To Understand Ant Financial*], 27 October 2014, <http://zennew.baijia.baidu.com/article/33845>

reference number) to transfer the money into the payee's bank account.

Currently, most online service providers add more functions onto their payment systems, for example, Alipay now has both payment and wallet functions that are linked to Alibaba's investment products. The main operators who run pure payment systems now (without additional functions) are only traditional banks' online portals and credit card providers who have online payment functions. In China, providing this service requires the Payment Services License on Non-financial Institutions.[24] However, the most popular pure online payment system, Unionpay Online,[25] does not need this licence.

2. Online Wallet

Wallet services are a development from payment systems. When service providers developed their own payment services in order to obtain greater deposits, these providers allowed users to retain balances in their transaction accounts, rather than transferring those funds back to their bank accounts. When the user makes his or her next online purchase, that balance can be used for the subsequent transaction. The development of Alipay is a good example on how a direct payment services developed into wallet services.

Most platforms involved in online sales of goods and services now have their own wallet service. For example, Apple[26] and Samsung,[27] as mobile devices producers, have introduced wallet services for their customers to purchase apps on their virtual stores. In China, Alipay, Wechat wallet (a payment function linked to Wechat accounts) and Baidu Wallet[28] are the most popular wallet services, all of which are similar with a balance maintenance function that aims to make user's online purchasing more convenient.

---

24 Issued by the Departments of Industry and Commerce.
25 中国银联在线支付 [Union Pay Online] (2 Apr 2016) <http://cn.unionpay.com/xinjiang/xinjiangservice/qitafuwu/file_77347815.html>.
26 Apple Pay (2 Apr 2016) <http://www.apple.com/apple-pay/>.
27 Samsung Pay (2 Apr 2016) < http://www.samsung.com/us/samsung-pay/>.
28 百度钱包 [Baidu Wallet] (2 Apr 2016) <https://www.baifubao.com/>.

3. Instalments

There are also online purchasing related services allowing users to pay for their purchased goods. Buyers can enjoy a good or service immediately without full payment. When a buyer applies to pay by instalments, the service provider will require their customer to set up an instalment account, and evaluate the risk level of that customer. The evaluation depends on the customer's financial situation and credit record for online purchases. As a result, the service provider sets a purchase limit for the customer to pay by instalments. Most instalment providers do not require customers to pay interest during the instalment period.

Currently, the two major online shopping platforms, Taobao (run by Alibaba) and JD are both providers of instalment payment systems, which are Taobao Instalment and JD Baitiao[29] respectively. More recently, JD Baitiao introduced its virtual credit card by cooperating with China CITIC Bank, which allows users to pay-up their purchase in a maximum 80-day period.[30] This is the first instance of combining a credit card with an instalment service, and it is the first credit card that was jointly provided by an E-Finance operator.

4. Direct Online Borrowing and Lending

The process of online borrowing and lending is the same as its counterpart in the real world. The only distinction is that the providers are all digital financial businesses, which leads to differences in evaluating the risk of customers. Services providers will require their borrower to upload their personal information, reasons of borrowing and the information on security. All these processes can be finished online without any site inspections, as borrowers are required to provide sufficient evidence about their credit level.

The best example on an E-Finance operator providing direct lending to its clients is JD Debt,[31] which initially only allowed sellers using JD as

---

29 京东白条, [Jingdong Baitiao] (2 Apr 2016) <http://baitiao.jd.com/>.
30 邓相 [Xiang DENG], 《京东联手中信银行推'小白'信用卡'》 [JD and CITIC Bank's Cooperation, 'Xiao Bai Ka' Credit Card] (3 Mar 2016) <http://soft.zol.cn/537/5374623.html> .
31 J.D. Debt (2 Apr 2016) <http://loan.jd.com/jdd.html>.

their platform to borrow money from JD. Now the availability of JD debt has extended to any JD user who is deemed to be reliable.

5. Money Market Fund

A money market fund is a very flexible type of low risk mutual fund.[32] This type of fund frequently pays returns with flexible rates. The characteristics of this type of fund are high levels of stability and high levels of flexibility, very similar to bank savings accounts. These products are widely used in the E-Finance market as a replacement for bank savings accounts. Some providers allow users to transfer their money from the online wallet into the money market fund to obtain higher income. Since the fund is flexible, money can easily be moved, and it has had a significant impact on the volume of short-term deposits in banks.

This type of product is not only being provided by fund companies and other financial institutions, but also by E-Finance operators. Yu'E Bao[33] provided by Ant Financial, and JD Treasury products[34] provided by JD, are two good examples of online money market funds where customers can deposit their money into wallets and transfer that money into a money market fund. The yield is paid on a daily basis. Supplying this type of service requires a financial services permit from the banking regulator.

6. Consumer Finance

According to China's 'Consumer Finance Companies Pilot Management Measures'[35], consumer finance enterprises are allowed to offer various types of financial services. The most important one related to this chapter is that these enterprises are allowed to lend money to individuals for consumption purposes.[36] The consumption purposes here do not include purchasing real estate and motor vehicles.[37] It is a very good way for E-Finance operators

---

32 U.S. Securities and Exchange Commission, 'Money Market Funds' (16 January 2013) <http://www.sec.gov/answers/mfmmkt.htm>.

33 余额宝 [Yu'Ebao] (2 Apr 2016) <https://financeprod.alipay.com/fund/index.htm>.

34 京东小金库 [JD Treasury] (2 Apr 2016) < http://xjk.jr.jd.com/index.htm>.

35 China Banking Regulatory Authority, 《消费金融公司试点管理办法》 [Consumer Finance Companies Pilot Management Measures, No.2] (2013).

36 Ibid Article 20.

37 Ibid Article 3.

to get involved in the debt market, especially for those who do not have banking licenses. Also, providing such services is helpful for those operators with e-commerce shopping platforms to increase their sales volume. For example, JD provides their 'JD tiny Debts'[38] to its customers who want to purchase relatively expensive goods online.

7. Crowd Funding[39] Platforms

This is a type of E-Finance service with relatively fewer financial characteristics. The process of obtaining 'crowd funding' is the fund-raiser publishes his or her idea or design project for a specific item (it can be a product, design or even a charity event) on the platform provided by E-Finance providers; then other users of the platform view those projects and can contribute money into the project.

All projects have a pre-set target for fund raising, and once the funds raised achieve that target, the fundraiser publishes that they are successful for getting that support from platform users. In return, the fundraiser sends the pre-committed rewards (can be anything other than currency) to those who funded the project. The E-Finance operator as the platform provider, only charges a fee from fundraisers whose project was successful in the crown funding process. As of March 2016, there is no mandatory financial-related license required for providing this type of service.

JD and Alibaba are the two largest platform providers for crowd funding. JD's platform is more close-ended: it is selective with the programs that it publishes, and those programs considered to be of poor quality will not be published. Alibaba's Taobao Crowd Funding is more open-ended which allows the public to publish and access to all types of programs, unless it is made illegal, regardless of the quality of such projects.

8. Financial Agent Service

Nearly all digital financial operators are currently offering this type of service as it is the one with the least regulatory requirements, as well as the lowest operating risks. Securities and fund management companies pay

---

38 京小贷 [JD Tiny Debt] (2 Apr 2016) < loan.jd.com/home.html>.
39 This refers to '众筹'.

these operators service fees be on the E-Finance operators' websites, while the operators themselves merely playing the role of intermediary. Running such services only requires a financial services agent license issued by the Department of Industry and Commerce; which is relatively easy to obtain.

Nearly all operators in the E-Finance market, no matter their size or other types of services provided, are providing agent services. For example, Alibaba's ZhaocaiBao[40] and Tencent Finance's LicaiTong[41].

Traditional Banking and the Internet

There are two comparative disadvantages for banks in competition with the new E-Finance operators: services-related weaknesses and the level of regulatory control.

Services-related Weaknesses

Banks in China interact with the Internet in two ways: 'Banking + Internet' and 'Internet + Banking', where 'Internet + Banking' is equivalent to E-Finance.

Banking + Internet is where banks provide their customers 24-hour online banking services anytime, anywhere with Internet Banking. Most banks have already launched their online banking and mobile banking services. Since 2013, many banks in China have also set-up direct banking platforms to expand their customer base and reduce human resource cost. The Internet allows banks to release new products, such as POS loan, where risk assessment is made based on transaction flow data provided by UnionPay.

Banking + Internet means banks cooperating with Internet companies. For example, the Industrial Bank established a strategic partnership with Ant Financial for mutual benefit and sustainable development.[42] The bank distributed loans to small & medium enterprises (SMEs) and the Internet companies provided information about the enterprises' operation status. Once these two institutions merged, banks could gain a list of en-

---

40 招财宝 [Zhaocai Bao] (2 Apr 2016) < https://zhaocaibao.alipay.com/pf/productList. htm>.

41 理财通 [Licai Tong] (2 Apr 2016) < https://qian.qq.com/>.

42 Ant Financial (2 Apr 2016) <http://www.antgroup.com/>.

terprises with good credit, active transaction activity and good development prospects. Likewise, those enterprises operating on Alibaba's e-commerce platform benefited by gaining access to financing from the banks.

Banks however should to more. In addition to actively adapting to the Internet, banks should provide personalised products and services, allowing customers to customise financial products according to their needs. Providing a free combination of various financial services, such as standardised credit rating tools, which automatically determine both lenders' and borrowers' credit ratings. Products and services provided by banks should not be confined to the traditional deposit, loan and exchange products, but also to integrate into people's daily lives. Forecasting customer demand and providing the necessary financial services, for example, to introduce a nearby restaurant based on customer lunch preferences.

To provide these services, banks need to use big data and cloud computing technologies to observe and predict customer needs. It is always difficult for SMEs to obtain finance in China. To ease this situation, an inclusive financial system has become the focus of future development of China's banking sector. Huaxia Bank,[43] with its experience of SMEs, is committed to providing the best fit for the needs of SMEs. Identifying the market position of banks, and building core competitiveness, is one of the trends in the banking industry.

Conclusion and Regulatory Issues

Another important reason that the digital financial operators enjoy such fast development in the last two decades is that there are limited regulations and supervision from the government. During the conference of CPPCC[44] the CEO of China Construction Bank (CCB) claimed that banks are a 'vulnerable group' in the financial market.[45] The reason the CEO was saying this is, as compared with other operators, especially the E-Finance operators, there are too many regulations and compliance requirements that banks have to follow. In China, the Banking Regulatory

---

43 华夏银行 [Huaxia Bank] (2 Apr 2016) < http://www.hxb.com.cn/home/cn/>.
44 Chinese People's Political Consultative Conference.
45 李学仁, 熊争艳 [Xueren LI and Zhengyan XIONG], above n 3.

Commission[46], Securities Regulatory Commission[47]and Insurance Regulatory Commission[48] are in charge of supervising the banking, securities and insurance sector respectively, and there are laws in relation to each sector of financial services. However, since E-Finance is a new segment in the financial sector, there were neither laws and regulations nor supervising authority to monitor it. This resulted in a very profitable, but sometimes risk-taking, digital financial industry; and it is clear that regulation-related costs for digital financial operators are much lower than for the traditional financial operators.

As a result, China's government has clearly found the necessity of setting-up regulations and supervising authorities. For example, the new *Consumer Finance Companies Pilot Management Measures*[49] was issued at the time that online consumption based finance had just begun to occur. Another good example of the Government attempting to supervise risky digital financial practices is the case in March 2014 of the central bank of China issuing a proscription to stop the 'Virtual Credit Card' that was jointly provided by Alibaba and China CITIC Bank.[50]

All these signs are showing that although there were no sufficient regulations and supervision by the Government before, the Chinese Government is trying to make regulations as well as getting more involved in the digital financial market.

---

46 中国银监会 [China Banking Regulatory Commission] (2 Apr 2016) <http://www.cbrc.gov.cn/index.html>.

47 Ibid.

48 Ibid.

49 China Banking Regulatory Authority, above n 35.

50 东平 [Ping DONG], 《央行叫停虚拟信用卡》 [*Central Bank ban the 'Virtual Credit Card'*], China Stock, 14 March 2014, <http://ggjd.cnstock.com/company/scp_ggjd/tjd_ggkx/201403/2947897.htm> (2 Apr 2016).

Chapter 6

Legal Risks of Online Platforms in China

Zhaozhao Wu

In September 2014, Alibaba completed the world's largest IPO in history at the New York Stock Exchange: US $25 billion.[1] In the lead up to this, Alibaba had seemingly emerged from obscurity to beat Amazon and eBay, becoming the largest online platform with annual sales of US $240 billion.[2] The publicity has not stopped since. On 23 January 2015, the China State Administration of Industry and Commerce (SAIC) published the findings of a survey carried out on Taobao.com, the C2C platform of Alibaba. Only 37.25 per cent of the products sampled proved to be genuine. Despite the defence it put forward to challenge the findings, Alibaba's stock price was penalised for this lingering problem as well as accusations levelled of being a primary enabler of counterfeiting products in China.[3]

The controversy did not stop Alibaba's continuing success with promoting its trademarked shopping festival – Double 11 or Singles' Day in 2015, the equivalent of Black Friday or Cyber Monday in concept but with

---

1 Ryan Mac, 'Alibaba Claims Title for Largest Global IPO Ever with Extra Share Sales', *Forbes* (online), 22 September 2014 <http://www.forbes.com/sites/ryanmac/2014/09/22/alibaba-claims-title-for-largest-global-ipo-ever-with-extra-share-sales/>.
2 Paul Mozur and Juro Osawa, 'Alibaba 11.11 Shopping Festival Breaks Record', *Wall Street Journal* (online), 11 November 2013 <http://www.wsj.com/articles/SB10001424052702304644104579191590951567808>.
3 Russell Flannery, 'Alibaba Is Facing Class Action Suit Tied To Dispute With China Regulators Over Fakes', *Forbes* (online), 31 January 2015 <http://www.forbes.com/sites/russellflannery/2015/01/31/alibaba-is-facing-class-action-suit-tied-to-dispute-with-china-regulators-over-fakes/>.

a gross merchandise volume (GMV) that neither Black Friday nor Cyber Monday will ever match. The reported one-day sales figure on 11 November 2015 exceeded US $18.8 billion, and 678 million parcels were delivered for the sales made on Singles' Day. Consumers from more than 211 countries and areas made orders via the online platforms in China during the 24 hours of the festival. The GMV doubled from the figures in 2014.[4] The scale, reach and growth rate of the development of online platforms can only be described as phenomenal.

While the e-commerce industry was still celebrating this new record, the China National Development and Reform Commission (NDRC) published a report to expose the major problem overshadowing the Alibaba Phenomenon. The reported incidents of counterfeit products accounted for 44.82 per cent of all transactions made during the shopping festival, an increase of 18.2 per cent from the previous year. The complaints regarding counterfeit items were concentrated in the sale of electronic gadgets (35.28 per cent). This result is particularly frustrating because Tmall, the B2C platform of Alibaba, was developed out of concerns that consumers had started to lose confidence when shopping for electronic products online.[5] Mechanisms – such as verifying the identification cards or industrial and commercial registration information of sellers, and accessing the China Compulsory Certification database – have been set-up to weed out counterfeit goods and boost the credibility of the online platform.[6] The efforts seem futile at this stage.

The second largest problem identified by the report was fictitious transactions. Alibaba has developed a credit system where an online seller will build up its credit by accumulating transactions with positive feed-

---

4 中国国家发展和改革委员会 [National Development and Reform Commission], 《2015年'双11'综合信用评价报告》 [Comprehensive Credit Report on Double 11, 2015], 29 December 2015.

5 Meng Jing, 'Alibaba Plans to Overhaul Its Image by Hosting Top Brands', *China Daily*, 8 December 2015.

6 丁壮 [Ding Zhuang], 《阿里与认监委信息中心合作 打通3C认证数据库》 [Alibaba Gains Access to China Compulsory Certificate in Cooperation with Certification and Accreditation Administration], 新浪科技 [*Sina Technology*], 24 December 2015 <http://tech.sina.com.cn/i/2015-12-24/doc-ifxmxxsr3606102.shtml>.

back. The credits are classified into different levels and displayed as a badge on its online shop front as well as on each product page. Consumers may rely on the information displayed to make a purchase choice. The fictitious transactions are abusing this system to boost a store's credits, misleading prospective consumers with deceptive information. In 2015, fictitious transactions jumped from 9.09 per cent to 18.57 per cent.[7]

The problems exposed by the report have called for the legislature to bring e-commerce law back on the agenda. The current regulatory framework for e-commerce in China is lagging behind the rapid development of e-commerce activities, transactions and platforms. Market and dispute resolutions rely heavily on limited provisions scattered in traditional consumer, torts and contract laws. The only legislative instrument that deals directly with the subject matter of e-commerce in a systemic way and sets out minimum requirements by which online platforms must abide is the *Stipulation on Development of Transactional Rules of Third-Party Platforms for Network Retailing (Trial Implementation)*. As the name suggests, the Stipulation is still in its trial phase. It is implemented by the Chinese Ministry of Commerce through central government order, making it merely a source of subsidiary legislation. The temporary and secondary nature of the legislation allows for greater flexibility in dealing with the rapidly changing e-commerce landscape. However, it also increases commercial uncertainty and legal risks for businesses and platform operators.[8]

With the government reluctant to take legislative initiative, the rules developed and imposed by digital platforms have become a substitute for the necessary legal infrastructure that regulates the tremendous amount of transactions taking place. These transactional rules are generally referred to as 'terms and conditions of the website', 'terms of use' or 'terms of service agreement'. They cover a broad range of issues including, but not limited to, eligibility of users, obligations and risk allocation, intellectual property protection, credit ratings, marketing standards, privacy policies and penal-

7 中国国家发展和改革委员会 [National Development and Reform Commission], above n 4.
8 薛军 [Xue Jun], 《电子商务立法框架和疑难问题研讨会》 [Seminar on Legal Framework and Challenges Associated with E-Commerce], Peking University E-Commerce Research and Development Foundation, 20 December 2014.

ties for contravention. To some extent, there is an overlap of topics between the terms of use and various legislative instruments. On the one hand, the concurrency provides the legitimate origin for such self-developed governing systems. On the other, any deviation in interpreting legislation and the corresponding transactional rules exposes the digital platforms to more legal risks. Some of the rules, especially the ones that limit the liability of digital platforms and increase costs for consumers to maintain their rights, have been challenged in court and read down by judges.

This chapter aims to analyse the role of terms of use and the legislative intention and judicial inclination towards e-commerce. In conclusion, focusing on the interaction between rules and legislation, the chapter will propose an optimal pathway for digital platforms to minimise legal risks and preserve a robust online free market that also has a sustainable self-regulating system to retain consumers.

Terms of Use

Terms of use are generally developed by digital platforms themselves. Such agreements are fundamentally based on years of online market-regulating practice. However, compared to other social norms, terms of use are relatively young. Even the most advanced regulatory system for online platforms only has a 10-year history.[9]

Before diving into the clause-by-clause analysis of terms of use, understanding the nature of digital platforms will help determine the role that terms of use play in reality.

1. The role of digital platforms

The business model for most digital platforms can be summarised as displaying platform users' product information, providing pay-for-performance marketing services, facilitating online transactions, charging commissions on transactions and storefront fees. There have been different schools of theories about the role and nature of online platforms.

---

9 唐远雄, 邱泽奇 [Tang Yuanxiong and Qiu Zeqi], 《淘宝平台规则的共生演化》 [The Evolution of Taobao Platform Rules], Beijing University China Sociology and Anthropology Research Centre.

The neutrality theory has deemed a digital platform as a third party that is independent from the transactions that occur on the platform.[10] Essentially, it is an internet information system provider that makes information about goods and services available to its users, enables and facilitates transactions, but never participates in the transaction directly or positively. This is the approach taken by the Chinese Ministry of Commerce in the *Stipulations on Development of Transactional Rules of Third-Party Platforms for Network Retailing* (the Stipulations).[11] It has some attributes similar to the ones of an Internet Services Provider (ISP). A platform, like an ISP, is not the content provider and therefore not held liable for content that might be tortious. A seller using the platform's services enters into a sale contract in its own name with a buyer. It holds out for its products and services using its own credentials, and is responsible for the sales, warranty and after-sale services.

To ensure the platforms' neutrality, the SAIC implements a set of Regulations on Network Transactions to further require a platform to clearly label its own direct transactional business offered on the platform.[12] If the platform fails to meet the labeling obligation, a consumer is allowed to rely on the assumption that they have been contracting with the platform directly where there is confusion.[13]

However, the current law's ambit stops short of dealing with the practical question of whether platforms should be held liable for the content

---

10 Hong Xue, 'Regulation of E-Commerce Intermediaries: An International Prospective' in Joao Ribeiro and Muruga Ramaswamy (eds.), *Trade Development through the Harmonisation of Commercial Law* (New Zealand Association for Comparative Law, October 2014).

11 In the definition of third party platforms in Article 3.2 of the 'Stipulations on Development of Transactional Rules of Third Party Platforms for Network Retailing', the third party e-commerce platforms refer to the information network system that provide transactional facilities and related services for both parties or multiple parties in an e-commerce transaction.

12 State Administration for Industry and Commerce, *Administrative Measures for Online Trading* (26 January 2014).

13 See further, in *Wang v Beijing Dangdang Information Technology Co Ltd* (March 2013) Beijing Chaoyang District People's Court, Civil First Instance 1596, 27 March 2013 where the court held that the invoice issued by Dangdang created a misleading and deceptive representation that the consumers were dealing with the platform directly and they were induced to buy the counterfeit products from a seller on the platform.

they are paid to promote. The major revenue for platforms comes from commissions charged on each transaction made on the platform. In promoting transactions, the issue of whether the platforms' neutrality is compromised remains.

An alternative theory is that the online platforms have an intermediary liability for third-party content or communications. The idea originates from the analogy to other Internet intermediaries that host, transmit, index, and provide access to content, products and services of third parties.[14] The Internet intermediaries are not the content providers. However, they make a profit by providing free content and services alongside advertising or branding/co-branding messages leveraging the volume of viewer traffic. As Internet intermediaries, their roles include:[15]

- Providing the infrastructure;
- Collecting, organising and evaluating dispersed information;
- Facilitating information exchange;
- Aggregating supply and demand;
- Facilitating market process;
- Providing trust; and
- Fulfilling the needs of buyers and sellers.

The element of trust is the key to the intermediary liability, despite the lack of a direct contractual relationship between a digital platform and its users.[16] The search results generated by the algorithms implemented on

---

14 Karine Perset, *The Economic and Social Role of Internet Intermediaries* (April 2010) Organisation of Economic Cooperation and Development <https://www.oecd.org/internet/ieconomy/44949023.pdf>.

15 Ana Rosa del Aguila-Obraa, Antonio Padilla–Melendeza and Christian Serarols–Tarresb, 'Value Creation and New Intermediaries on Internet. An Exploratory Analysis of the Online News Industry and the Web Content Aggregator' (2007) 27(3) *International Journal of Information* 187.

16 See further: *Chen v Beijing Dangdang Information Technology Co. Ltd.*, Beijing Chaoyang District People's Court, Civil First Instance No. 16367, 14 March 2013, where the court held that the consumer bought the counterfeit mobile phones in good faith and by relying on the platform provider's representation that only genuine products were sold on the platform. This representation was reinforced by the platform provider's promise of compensation at five times the purchase price.

digital platforms can be deemed as the recommendation of the platforms. This recommendation is remunerated by the number of consumers clicking on the ads.[17] Most jurisdictions impose an intermediary liability if the platforms have actual or constructive knowledge of the activities of third parties who have paid for the services provided by online platforms.[18] This theory has been adopted by the legislature in China and is reflected in new amendments to the *Consumer Protection Law* in China where Article 44 sets out:

> Providers of online transaction platforms that know or should know that sellers or service providers use their platforms to infringe upon the legitimate rights and interests of consumers but fail to take necessary measures shall bear joint and several liability with the sellers or service providers in accordance with the law.[19]

However, the law is not clear about how to establish actual or constructive knowledge, and the defence of necessary measures. As a consequence, the courts are not consistent in applying the safe harbour principle and this increases the legal risks for digital platforms in China.[20] Where the law is silent, the secondary source relied on by the courts are private treaties (contracts) between the parties.

---

17 谢冬敏 [Xie Dongmin], 《第三方交易平台法律责任浅析》 [Analysis of Third-party Transactional Platform's Legal Responsibilities] *China Industry and Commerce News*, 24 November 2014.

18 Ignacio Garrote Fernandez-Diez, Comparative Analysis on National Approaches to the Liability of Internet Intermediaries for Infringement of Copyright and Related Rights (30 April 2014), WIPO Standing Committee on Copyright and Related Rights <http://www.wipo.int/export/sites/www/copyright/en/doc/liability_of_internet_intermediaries_garrote.pdf>.

19 《中华人民共和国消费者权益保护法》 [Law of the People's Republic of China on the Protection of Consumer Rights and Interests] (People's Republic of China) Article 44.

20 *E-Land (Shanghai Fashion Trade Co Ltd v Zhejiang Taobao Network Co. Ltd and Du Guofa*, Shanghai Pudong New District People's Court, Civil (Intellectual Property) First Instance No.426 9 January 2011, where the court held that the mere deletion of infringing links upon notice does not suffice as necessary measures. A digital platform needs to take effective and reasonable measures in its capacity of marketplace management. In *Nippon Paint Co Ltd v Zhanjin Company and Taobao*, Shanghai Xuhui District People's Court, October 2011, the court found that notice and takedown was sufficient to invoke the safe harbour defence.

Practically speaking, terms of use govern most of the legal issues that a consumer will encounter from registration as a user until post-sale services. For example, as the most advanced and sophisticated online regulatory system, the terms of use developed by Alibaba, also known as the Taobao rules, have four broad categories of terms: eligibility, marketing, transaction, and penalty. These are the pillar regulations that govern and facilitate the transactions of 367 million buyers who can use the biggest e-commerce platform with peace of mind, while waiting for the e-commerce law to be drafted.[21] The significance of the terms of use can never be overestimated.

2. The role of terms of use

Traditionally, the terms of use have been simplified as the contract between a platform and its users. However, various issues arise when applying contract law principles to the terms of use.

The first issue is the doctrine of privity.[22] Generally, the terms of use outline a set of contractual relationships:

- A service agreement between a platform and consumers;
- A service agreement between a platform and businesses; and
- Sales of goods or services agreements between businesses and consumers subject to the service agreements they have with the platform respectively.

Inevitably, the terms of use will confer rights and impose obligations on both businesses and consumers who are using the platform to conclude a sales agreement. However, the doctrine of privity does not allow a consumer or a business to enforce the terms of use directly in a court proceeding. It has become a platform's responsibility to administrate the terms of use and the conduct of its users. Under these circumstances, upholding the

---

21 施志军 [Shi Zhijun], 《电商法草案有望年内完成，第三方平台规则或纳入》 [E-commerce Law is Likely to Finish Drafting Within the Year and Incorporate the Rules of Third Party Transactional Platforms], 京华时报 [*Beijing Times*], 26 August 2015.

22 This is an established principle in common law countries because of *Tweddle v Atkinson*. Privity is also recognised in civil law countries, including China. Article 8 of the Contract Law of the People's Republic of China has also incorporated the same doctrine.

neutrality theory will look like a ploy for platforms to shift their liabilities. If a platform is not purely a contractual party in this legal triangle, other questions arise: for instance, how does a contract give a platform the power to impose punitive measures on its counterparties;[23] and what is in the contract to ensure that a platform will carry out its administrative duties with competency and fairness? These questions are further exacerbated in the second issue.

The second challenge is the prevalent use of a 'not entire agreement clause' in terms of use. It has become the general practice to include a clause in the terms of use that expressly provides that the contract is formed, but the content of the contract is not limited to the current terms of use alone. Platforms have the right to add, remove and vary the terms of use, and by continuing to use the platform services, a user agrees to be bound by the new terms of use.[24] This fundamentally disrupts the doctrine of *consensus ad idem*: a contract cannot be amended without a consensus by all parties.[25] Such a term might be read down by the courts *contra proferentem* to disallow a party from unilaterally changing a standard form contract to impose more obligations on the other party or more stringent requirements for the other party to exercise their rights.[26] Such a term has also been regarded as an unfair contract term and excluded from operative clauses in the common law system.[27]

The justification for digital platforms to keep the right to make unilateral changes is that the online marketplace is constantly evolving and

---

23 In particular, Alibaba's terms of use provide for termination of the use of the platform permanently for breach. It will have a catastrophic effect on the livelihood for businesses that have built their entire operation online. Given the market share of Alibaba, it potentially amounts to a denial of market access, which is a violation of anti-competition law in China.

24 史宇航 [Shi Yuhang], 《网络用户协议的法律研究》 [Legal Analysis of Online Terms of Use] (8 February 2012) AliResearch <http://www.aliresearch.com/blog/article/detail/id/14495.html>.

25 Contract Law of The People's Republic of China (People's Republic of China), Article 77.

26 孙良国 [Sun Liangguo], 《单方修改合同条款的公平控制》 [Fair Control of the Right to Unilaterally Amend A Contract] (2013) 1 《法学》 *Law Science Monthly*.

27 For instance, in the Australian Consumer Law, a unilateral variation clause that may cause a significant imbalance in the rights of the parties to the contract is an unfair contract term. See further, in *Director of Consumer Affairs Victoria v AAPT Limited* [2006] VCAT 1493.

the services a platform can provide are changing every day.[28] It is just and equitable for the service providers to change the terms of use to manage their risks and lower their costs. If a platform has to renegotiate with every user when its circumstances have changed, the process would be very costly and eventually the end users would bear the increased costs. It has been proposed that the court should apply the test if there are sufficient resultant remedies for the users,[29] but it also means that the court will have to look at the particular circumstances of each case to weigh legitimate business interests against the necessity to uphold the contract. The result might differ from case to case. To reduce the risk of its own terms of use being struck down by the courts,[30] online platforms should start thinking about reconceptualising the terms of use as something more than a contract.

If it is not a simple contract, what could it be? The terms of use are defined by the Chinese Ministry of Commerce as 'public rules provided, amended and implemented by a third-party platform operator, applicable to non-specified subjects using the platform services, and involving social public interest.'[31] The administration further mandates the following subject matters must be included in the terms of use of a platform's:

- eligibility to register a user account;
- transactional rules;
- confidentiality and privacy policy;
- dispute resolution;

---

28 屠世超，林国华 [Tu Shichao and Lin Guohua], 《网络服务用户协议的效力探析》 [Analysing the Effect of Online Terms of Use], (2008) 4 《电子商务月刊》 *E-Business Journal*.

29 Chinese Ministry of Commerce, Stipulation on Development of Transactional Rules of Third-Party Platforms for Network Retailing (Trial Implementation) (24 December 2014), Article 7.

30 The court in *Bei En E-commerce Co Ltd v Zhejiang Taobao Network Co Ltd*, Shandong Jinan Intermediate People's Court, Economic Appeal No. 566, 20 July 2015, held that the jurisdiction clause in the terms of use is void due to its violation of Article 40 of the Contract Law of the People's Republic China. The jurisdiction clause in a standard form contract will impose an unnecessary burden for the recipient of the contract to enforce their rights.

31 Above n 29, Article 3.

- governing law and jurisdiction;
- liability.[32]

Interestingly, online platforms are also obliged to provide, amend and implement a set of by-laws on top of the terms of use. Despite the different terminology, there are obvious overlapping subject matters in both the terms of uses and by-laws:

- Eligibility to register a user account;
- Transactional rules;
- Disclosure of information and approval regimes;
- Confidentiality and privacy policy;
- Consumer protection;
- Advertisement review;
- Transaction security and date backup;
- Dispute resolution;
- Spam reporting;
- Other rules required by law.[33]

It is also a platform's responsibility to take active measures to improve the administration of these by-laws. At first sight, these secondary regulations suggest that the government is making platforms responsible for protecting their users against irregularities that arise from using the platforms' services. They are conferring more regulatory discretion that is supposed to be vested in the executive arm of the government. This may cause concern about the legitimacy of such authorisation in terms of administrative law. However, it is an invaluable opportunity for platforms to redeem themselves and reduce the legal risks by passing the code of conduct/by-law/self-regulatory rules that are in compliance with the expectations of the government. There still remains an issue of how to make sure that the interests of both businesses and consumers are addressed even-handedly in terms of use, given that there is no guarantee of the neutrality of platforms as a regulator as well as an administrator.

32 Chinese Ministry of Commerce, *Regulation on Services of Third-Party E-commerce Transactional Platforms* (12 April 2011), Article 5.7.
33 Above n 32, Article 5.6.

This issue has proved to be very critical, as the Taobao New Rules Incident in 2011 has put the whole mechanism to a test. On 10 October 2011, Tmall, the B2C department of Alibaba announced that a new rule was introduced to increase the annual fee for businesses who continue to use the platform from ￥6,000 to ￥30,000 or ￥60,000, depending on the size of the business. The security deposit would also rise from ￥10,000 up to ￥150,000. Another new rule was to allow Alibaba to claim for liquidated damages against the security bond for at least ￥10,000 if a business breached the terms of use. The forfeited bond would be funnelled into a fund used to compensate consumers who have suffered loss or damage from a business' breach of the terms of use. A consumer is entitled to as much compensation as five times the purchase price, if the products they bought are found to be counterfeit, unauthorised goods, parallel imports or made from counterfeiting material compositions.[34] It is a strategic move for Alibaba to whitewash the lack of consumer protection in the terms of use and make small businesses bear the costs.

The small vendors sought frontier justice by taking the protest to the platform. An Anti-Taobao Coalition was formed of approximately 40,000 small vendors and organised attacks on large vendors on Alibaba. They placed massive orders with top vendors on the platform with no intention to buy but to cancel the orders and ask for refunds. In addition, they manipulated the rating system by giving false and poor reviews. The vendors under attack had no choice but to take down their products and suspend their business temporarily. It is reported that some of the large vendors suffered a loss of up to RMB 10 million during the attack.[35]

As this was potentially a cybercrime, Alibaba reported the attack to the police and promised to compensate the victims of the attacks in order to retain their business. On October 15, the Department of Electronic Com-

34 Doris Li, 'The Emergence and Development of Tmall' (2012) 48 *China Intellectual Property*.

35 Susan Ning, Liu Jia, Sun Yi Ming and Yin Ranran, *Tmall Incident – Another Chinese Internet Giant Accused of Abusing Dominance* (27 October 2011) Antitrust and Competition – King and Wood Mallesons <http://www.chinalawinsight.com/2011/10/articles/corporate/antitrust-competition/tmall-incident-another-chinese-internet-giant-accused-of-abusing-dominance>.

merce and Information of the Ministry of Commerce (MOFCOM) intervened as a mediator to conciliate the relationship breakdown between the platforms and its users whose interests had been profoundly jeopardised without prior consultation. On October 17, both parties reached a deal that Alibaba would delay the implementation of the new rules and handed over a ¥1.8 billion payout to support small businesses, and the whole incident finally came to a conclusion.[36]

In response to this incident, the Ministry of Commerce published the *Stipulation on Development of Transactional Rules of Third-Party Platforms for Network Retailing*, which requires that platforms provide 30 days' prior notice before changing any terms of use. Users are entitled to terminate the contract by serving a written notice within 60 days of platforms announcing their intended amendment of terms of use, and they are only bound by the terms of use effective prior to the termination.[37] The 30 days' prior notice and 60 days' rejection period provide the timeframe for platforms and their users to negotiate in good faith about the proposed changes to the terms of use. However, these stipulations are still based on the presumption that the terms of use are of a contractual nature and the doctrine of freedom of contract should be applied. However, the reality is that not everyone has a seat at the negotiating table. Small business and individual consumers in particular, who have no advocacy in the supposed negotiations, are left with two options, namely to take it or leave it. Therefore, in 2014, an additional protective scheme was introduced mandating a seven-day period for platforms to collect feedback and provide replies before any changes to the terms of use take effect.[38] If there is a material effect on the interests of businesses and consumers, platforms should implement transitional measures.[39] However, the regulation does not go into detail about what due process needs to be followed. Instead, it leaves great space for platforms to make up their own rules to comply with the regu-

---

36 Sabrina Mao and Ken Wills, 'China Small Business Owners Expand Fee Protest to Alipay', *Reuters* (online), 24 October 2011 <http://www.reuters.com/article/us-china-ali-pay-fees-idUSTRE79N13320111024>.

37 Above n 32, Article 5.8.

38 Above n 29, Article 7.

39 Above n 29, Article 10.

lation. The government's attitude, though somewhat ambiguous, has laid the foundation for an online self-regulation system. There are also severe consequences for failing to comply with the self-regulatory responsibilities. For instance, Article 19 of the Stipulation sets out that any adoption, amendment or implementation of terms of use violating the public interest will attract criminal punishment.[40] The management or officers of a platform may also be found personally liable for the criminal charges.[41]

To reduce the legal risks, digital platforms need to take pre-emptive action to establish explicit procedures and systems to ensure enforcement of the self-regulatory rules against market participants and supervision of their trading activities. The remaining question is where the law enforcement power comes from? It has become vital for digital platforms to achieve the legitimacy of self-regulation. There are normally three ways:

- Authorised by laws;
- Authorised by the administrator; and
- Agreements.[42]

To some extent, digital platforms have acquired legitimacy of self-regulation from the authorities through the government and via multilateral agreement. The legitimacy provided through law is the next milestone and there has been strong political will to pass a comprehensive e-commerce law to remove the uncertainty about the effectiveness of terms of use.

E-commerce Law

In 2013, the Financial and Economic Committee of the National People's Congress initiated the legislative process of e-commerce law. A special task force was set up to conduct industrial surveys, invite public submissions and promote focused discussion. Towards the end of 2015, a final draft of the e-commerce law was presented to the Financial and Economic Committee. It is scheduled for submission to an NPC standing committee

40 Above n 29, Article 19.
41 Above n 29, Article 21.
42 黎军[Li Jun], 《行业组织的行政法问题研究》 [Administration Law Problems with Trade Organsiations], 北京大学出版社 [Peking University Press], 2002.

for further reading and will be promulgated as early as 2017.[43]

A significant number of self-regulatory rules that have been implemented by platforms over the years – such as rules on the consumer protection fund, verification of business owners and credit rating system – have been recognised as trade practices and integrated in the draft e-commerce law.[44]

It is expected that the e-commerce law, once promulgated, will endorse digital platforms as the front-line regulator of their respective online marketplaces. It will provide the legitimacy required by a self-regulatory regime. However, it also manifests the issue of the hierarchy within the terms of use. Within a simplified hierarchy, there will be five broad categories of terms:

- Terms endorsed by e-commerce law or other primary statutes;
- Terms endorsed by secondary regulations;
- Terms agreed by all users or a majority of the users;
- Terms inconsistent with judicial interpretation; and
- Unfair or illegal terms.

How to resolve the competing terms has been an ongoing debate within the online community of users on the same platform and will become the next challenging legal research.

Conclusion

As the front-line regulator, platforms are responsible for filling the gaps where the legislative regime is lacking or lagging behind. The self-regulation approach has provided the flexibility for online platforms to implement new rules as required by the development of an online marketplace as well as to enforce the code of conduct to allocate limited valuable resources to high-risk areas. Within the self-regulation system, there are generally venues for low-cost alternative dispute resolution where the users are

---

43 薛军 [Xue Jun], 《电商法明年上半年望审议 或不涉互联网金融和税收》 [E-Commerce Law is Expected to be Reviewed in the First Half of 2016 and is Unlikely to Include Internet Finance and Tax], *Caijing Magazine*, 14 December 2015.

44 *Administrative Measures for Online Trading*, above n 12, Articles 26, 30, 33 and 36.

involved in applying the rules, which reinforce the awareness of abiding by the self-made regulations and the faith in the self-regulation system. It is a cost-effective method to monitor the trading activities of market participants, bring down the compliance costs for users and minimise the supervising costs for the government. Arguably, the financial costs of regulating online markets have been shifted from the government to digital platforms. It is still in the best interests of the platforms to reduce the legal risks by taking proactive measures to reduce administrative and judicial intervention. Self-regulation entitles digital platforms the defence of best endeavour if its self-regulatory duties are reasonably discharged.[45] The costs of maintaining a self-regulatory system should be internalised as part of the services and infrastructure provided by an online platform.

---

45 Cento Veljanovski, 'Economic Approaches to Regulation' in Robert Baldwin, Martin Cave and Martin Lodge (eds.), *The Oxford Handbook of Regulation: Theory, Strategy and Practice* (Oxford University Press, 2010) Ch. 2.

Chapter 7

Virtual Currency, Money Laundering Risks and Regulation

David Chaikin

In this chapter the fundamental characteristics of virtual currency, methods of classification and the variety of risks in virtual currency schemes will be analysed. Virtual currencies do not constitute legal tender in any jurisdiction, and have not been subject to regulation in regard to their issue, administration and redemption. The classification of virtual currency schemes is significant because of the implications for regulation. There are a variety of risks arising from virtual currencies, but recent focus has been on the potential for money laundering. The basic elements of money laundering will be analysed, with a view to understanding how virtual currency schemes facilitate financial crimes and money laundering. It will be argued that decentralised, convertible virtual currencies, such as bitcoin, pose the greatest risk for money laundering. The application of anti-money laundering laws will be briefly examined with a view to suggesting reform measures to limit the misuse of virtual currencies.

Characteristics of Virtual Currency

Virtual Currency (VC) schemes are a relatively new phenomena, with bitcoin being created in January 2009. VC has rapidly grown in size, purpose and usage over the past eight years, so that there are numerous VCs in circulation. It is estimated that there are over 700 VC schemes, with the most important being Bitcoin, Ethereum, Ripple and Lifecoin.[1] Bitcoin dominates the market, with 16.1 million units in circulation at a market capitalisation of $14.56 billion as at 16 January 2017.[2] These numbers are fluid because of the volatility of price changes of bitcoin units and the limited supply of bitcoins; for example, in the past year, market capitalisation has been as low as $6.16 billion. The main methods of acquiring VCs are either 'directly thorough mining, bilateral transactions with other investors, from a firm selling VCs, such as the purchase of options', or 'indirectly via a virtual currency exchange'.[3] There may be other ways of obtaining VCs, such as lending/borrowing VCs, using VCs as collateral, or through gifts.

The classification of VCs poses problems for regulators in that VCs 'combines properties of currencies, commodities and payment systems'.[4] The definitional challenge is exacerbated because a variety of terms are used in the virtual money space – 'crypto-currency', 'virtual currency', 'digital currency' – which cause confusion in the policy debate as to what is the most appropriate form of regulation. Developers prefer the term 'crypto-currency' which is backed by a cryptographic algorithm, facilitated and verified by a network of users (peer to peer), and is recorded on public online ledger (called the 'blockchain').[5] Many regulators favours the phrase 'virtual currency', defined as a 'type of unregulated, digital money, which is issued and usually controlled by its developers, and used and accepted among the members of a specific virtual community'.[6] The Financial Action Task Force (FATF) has adapted this definition by describing VC as a 'digital representation of value' that is not 'issued or guaranteed by

1 *Crypto-Currency Market Capitalizations* <https://coinmarketcap.com/>.
2 Blockchain, *Market Capitalization*, <https://blockchain.info/charts/market-cap>.
3 French Government, *Regulating Virtual Currencies*, Virtual Currencies Working Group, Ministry of Finance, Paris, June 2014, 3.
4 Dong He, Karl Habermeier, Ross Leckow, Vikram Haksar, Yasmin Alemeida, Mikari Kashima, Nadim Kyriakos-Saad, Hiroko Oura, Tahsin Saadi Sedik, Natalia Stetsenko, and Concepcion Verdugo-Yepes, *Virtual Currencies and Beyond: Initial Considerations*, Monetary and Capital Markets, Legal Strategy and Policy Review Departments, International Monetary Fund, Washington DC, January 2016, 24 <https://www.imf.org/external/pubs/ft/sdn/2016/sdn1603.pdf>.
5 He, above n 4, 9.
6 European Central Bank, *Virtual Currency Schemes*, ECB, Frankfur am Main, October 2012, <http://www.ecb.europa.eu/pub/pdf/other/virtualcurrencyschemes201210en.pdf>.

any jurisdiction', and may in some circumstances function as an alternative currency within a 'community of users'.[7]

The distinguishing feature of VC is its lack of legal monetary status in that it is not legal tender in any jurisdiction. It is not only the issue, transfer and redemption of VC that is not regulated, but also the issuer of the currency is not subject to supervision. Consequently, VC schemes are not subject to the gamut of domestic and international regulations that apply to real world currencies.

One way of understanding VC is to compare it to 'electronic money' (e-money) issued by established electronic money institutions.[8] E-money is a 'digital representation of fiat currency' (also known as 'national currency').[9] Virtual currency is similar to e-money in that both rely on a money format that is digital.[10] While e-money schemes use traditional currencies as their unit of account, VC schemes rely on an invented currency, such as bitcoin, which is not legal tender. This is significant because 'complete control of the virtual currency is left to its issuer, which is usually a non-financial private company',[11] that is not subject to effective supervision.

A VC has the potential to satisfy a number of the functions of money in that it can operate as a 'medium of exchange' or 'unit of account' in a specific virtual community, such as in an online gambling environment.[12] A VC scheme may also provide money functions in a virtual criminal community, such as the case of Liberty Reserve, which is discussed below. Whether a VC can also provide the 'store of value' functionality is yet to be determined. VC schemes are attractive because of their low transaction

7 FATF, *Virtual Currencies: Key Definitions and Potential AML/CTF Risks*, FATF, Paris June 2014, 4. See also European Central Bank, *Virtual Currency Schemes – a further analysis*, ECB, Frankfur am Main, February 2015, 25, <https://www.ecb.europa.eu/pub/pdf/other/virtualcurrencyschemesen.pdf>.

8 According to the EU Electronic Money Directive (2009/110/EC), 'electronic money' is 'monetary value as represented by a claim on the issuer which is: stored electronically; issued on receipt of funds of an amount not less in value than the monetary value issued; and accepted as a means of payment by undertakings other than the issuer'.

9 FATF, above n 7, 4.

10 European Central Bank, above n 6, 16–17 (discussion concerning the similarities and differences between virtual currency schemes and electronic money schemes).

11 Ibid 5.

12 Ibid 11.

costs, but this is counter balanced by the absence of government support. A VC scheme does not have the reputation for being a reliable and safe investment; its speculative status suggests that it does not provide a long-terms store of value for investors. Currently VC's are not widely acceptable as a medium of exchange because of a lack of trust and confidence by potential users. In practice, until VCs can 'attract a critical mass of users',[13] it is unlikely that VCs will become an alternative currency; nevertheless, VCs can present problems for users, investors and the wider financial system.[14]

VC schemes have been classified into various types based on their relationship with real money/real economy and the process of administration. The first method of classification distinguishes between a convertible/open scheme and a non-convertible/closed scheme. In a convertible VC, the VC will have an equivalent value in legal tender and can be exchanged for legal tender, whereas a non-convertible VC has no real world money equivalent. In theory, there is little governmental interest in non-convertible VC schemes where virtual goods and services are traded only in the virtual environment and there is no linkage to the real economy. Examples of non-convertible VC schemes are frequent flyer schemes or loyalty programs, or online games, such as World of Warcraft® (WoW) Gold. Because WOW Gold is purchased by players to use only within this online game, and cannot be exchanged for real value, it is unlikely to pose any serious regulatory challenges. However, as a black market could develop outside the VC scheme, regulators should monitor non-convertible VC schemes as they grow in popularity.[15] In contrast, in convertible VC schemes there are linkages to the real world economy, for example permitting the purchase and sale of VC tied to a real exchange rate, as well as the exchange of virtual and real goods and services. Examples of convertible VC schemes are bitcoin, or the Linden™ dollar issued by Second Life®, which may be purchased by using real currency, and may be sold in exchange for US dollars.

13 Dirk G Baur, Kihoon Hong and Adrian D Lee, *Virtual Currencies: Media of Exchange or Speculative Asset?* (29 June 2016) SWIFT Institute Working Paper No. 2014-007 <SSRN: https://ssrn.com/abstract=2803941>.
14 European Central Bank, above n 6, 17.
15 FATF, above n 7, 6.

Another method of classification of VCs schemes concerns the issue, control and administration of VCs. A distinction is drawn between VC schemes that are controlled by a single administrative authority (centralised VC) and those created by a community of users which are not subject to centralised administrative oversight (decentralised VC). Bitcoin is cited as an example of a decentralised VC system in that it has 'no central control, no central repository of information, no central management, and crucially, no central point of failure'.[16] The core idea of decentralisation is that there is no central or single organisation that acts as an issuer of VC or has the power to withdraw VC from circulation. In a decentralised VC scheme there is no gatekeeper or monitor to compel a person to use or exchange VC in a predetermined manner. Further, in a decentralised scheme, the 'validation and certification of transactions are performed by users of the system and therefore do not require a third party to perform intermediation activities'.[17] Decentralised VC schemes allow direct communications between users, thereby lowering transaction costs through disintermediation.

The attributes of VC schemes that are crypto-currencies which make them attractive to potential users, include:[18]

> The speed of transactions and low transaction costs arising from the 'nearly instantaneous transmission of value' using the Internet, 'without the need for a trusted third-party intermediary', such as a bank;

> The use of a decentralised system which 'provides network security and transaction verification' through public-private key cryptography and a public record;

---

16 Erik Voorhees, 'Is Bitcoin Truly Decentralized – Yes – and Here is Why It's Important', *Bitcoin Magazine*, 22 January 2015 <https://bitcoinmagazine.com/articles/bitcoin-truly-decentralized-yes-important-1421967133/>.

17 United States Government Accountability Office, *Virtual Currencies: Emerging Regulatory, Law Enforcement, and Consumer Protection Challenges*, Report to the Committee on Homeland Security and Government Affairs, US Senate, GAO-14-496 (29 May 2014) 5.

18 Pricewaterhouse Coopers LLP, *Money is no object: Understanding the evolving cryptocurrency market*, PWC Financial Services Institute, August 2015, 3 <http://www.pwc.com/us/en/financial-services/publications/assets/pwc-cryptocurrency-evolution.pdf>.

The avoidance of forgery or counterfeiting through the veri-fication of each transaction, which is posted to a global pub-lic transaction ledger or block chain; and

The ongoing development of the technology and its appli-cation by sophisticated developers and miners, who provide innovative input to 'improve the code, secure the network and validate transactions'.

It is the underlying technology of VC schemes, rather than the VC scheme per se, that has the greatest potential for economic advancement. The idea of block chain technology is that each transaction is recorded in a publicly distributed ledger, with a constant updating of records that face minimal risks of hacking or interference. The security and speed of the transactions occur in circumstances where the 'block chain is copied across the entire network of computers running the bitcoin software, and the owners of the computers do not necessarily know or trust one another'.[19] Described as 'the most important disruptor' in business and finance, the block chain technology has the potential to revolutionise industries, such as the payments and clearing systems in banking and finance, the securi-ties and financial instruments markets, the real estate market, as well as smart contracts and electoral systems. [20] Whether block chain technology reaches its potential is yet to be determined; there are a number of chal-lenges, both technological and human, that must be overcome before it will become successful.

Virtual Currency and Risks

VC schemes create new types of risks, including legal risk (in that the legal status of VC is largely unregulated or uncertain), credit risk (in that the value of VC fluctuates in accordance with demand and supply), and liquidity risk (in that there is no government guarantee of the possibility

19 Andy Extance, 'The future of cryptocurrencies: Bitcoin and beyond', (2015) 526(7571) *Nature* <http://www.nature.com/news/the-future-of-cryptocurrencies-bitcoin-and-be-yond-1.18447>.
20 Pricewaterhouse Coopers LLP, above n 18, 16.

of redeeming VCs even at par value).[21] Other risks include consumer/investment protection risk, network security risk, and prudential safety and soundness risk.[22] It has been suggested that VCs do not 'pose a material risk to monetary and financial stability',[23] but this is based on the assumption that VCs are unlikely to become a significant influence in the real world. The same assumption should not be made in relation to the potential criminal misuse of VCs, either through fraud or computer hacking at the expense of users, or through tax crimes and money laundering. This is because the demand for VCs includes not only 'technology enthusiasts' and 'investors/gamblers', but also financial criminals such as tax evaders and money launderers.[24]

Tax evasion and aggressive tax avoidance are important risks in VC schemes, given the secrecy features underlying VCs. Twenty years ago the ATO presciently identified anonymity in Internet payment systems as a critical issue for future tax compliance.[25] There is also the problem of lack of knowledge of tax issues arising from VC schemes. As the US Government Accountability Office (GAO) has stated where VC is used for the payment of goods and services, taxpayers may not realise that they are earning taxable income in the virtual environment, or understand how to calculate their taxable income. [26] In recent years tax authorities have given users of VC guidance on this subject, for example in 2014 the Australian Taxation Office (ATO) issued a guidance paper and draft rulings on various tax aspects of VCs, treating VCs as assets for capital gains purposes and Goods and Services Tax purposes.[27] The ATO guidance on GST

21 European Central Bank above n 6, 16.

22 FATF, *Guidance for a Risk-Based Approach:Virtual Currencies*, FATF, Paris, June 2015, 6–7; and He, above n 4, 24

23 Robleh Ali, John Barrdear, Roger Clews and James Southgate, 'The economics of digital currency', *Bank of England, Quarterly Bulletin*, 2014 Q3, 1.

24 Luc Laeven, *Virtual Currency Schemes*, Presentation at Chief Economists Workshop. Bank of England, London, 20 May 2015.

25 Australian Taxation Office, *Tax and the Internet*, vols 1 & 2, AGPS, Canberra, 1997.

26 United States Government Accountability Office, *Virtual Economies and Currencies: Additional IRS Guidance Could Reduce Tax Compliance Risks*, Report to the Committee on Finance, US Senate, Washington DC, GAO-13-516, 15 May 2013 <http://www.gao.gov/assets/660/654620.pdf>.

27 Australian Taxation Office, *Tax treatment of crypto-currencies in Australia – specifical-*

treatment of VCs was criticised by the Australian Senate, which recommended that VCs should be treated as a currency for the purposes of GST so that individuals would not be liable for GST when they buy VCs.[28] Closely related to the issue of tax evasion risk is money laundering risk which is discussed below.

Overview of Money Laundering

Money laundering is the process by which one conceals or disguises the true nature, source, disposition, movement or ownership of money. Money laundering is used to break the paper trail by, for example, using cash or transferring funds overseas to a tax haven or bank secrecy haven.[29] The purpose of money laundering is to create the appearance that illicit assets have a legitimate source, thereby preventing seizure and confiscation. Other purposes include the avoidance of detection by law enforcement to reduce the likelihood of prosecution for the substantive underlying (predicate) offence; it is the ownership and/or control of illicit assets that will connect the senior leadership of organised crime to the predicate offence[30]. Money laundering is often an element of predicate offences, such as drug trafficking, organised crime, terrorism, fraud and tax evasion. Where money laundering is detected and investigated so that illicit assets are traced, there is the possibility of freezing and confiscating such assets. Money laundering is a public global bad because it undermine financial stability, national security, and the political and social system. The International Monetary Fund estimates that Money Laundering is about 2-4% of the World's Gross Domestic Product, which amounts to trillions of dollar per year.[31]

The conventional methodology states that there are three stages in the money laundering process. First, placement involves the physical disposal

ly bitcoin, 18 December 2014, <https://www.ato.gov.au/General/Gen/Tax-treatment-of-crypto-currencies-in-Australia---specifically-bitcoin/>.

28 The Senate, *Digital Currency – Game changer or bit player*, Economics References Committee, Parliament of Australia, Canberra, Senator Sam Dastyari (Chair), August 2015, 28-35.

29 See David Chaikin, 'Money Laundering; 'An Investigatory Perspective' (1991) 2:1 *Criminal Law Forum* 467, 467–8.

30 Australian Crime Commission, *Organised Crime in Australia 2015*, Commonwealth of Australia, 2015, 9–10.

31 FATF, *Frequently Asked Questions*, FATF <http://www.fatf-gafi.org/faq/moneylaundering/>.

of proceeds of criminal activity, for example, the deposit of drug cash into a bank account. Second, layering involves the separating of illicit funds from their source through transactions that disguise or obscure the audit trail and provide secrecy for example, the transfer of funds through a series of corporate bank accounts in a number of countries. Third, integration involves the placing of laundered proceeds into the legitimate economy as normal funds, such as the repatriation of monies into the home country disguised as a foreign investment.

Applying the conventional stages of money laundering to the payments process, which may involve digital money, it has been said that the 3 stages 'can easily be combined at an information technology level through electronic means'.[32] For example, the sender in a virtual currency scheme may be able to transmit funds directly to the purchaser by using instruments which do not use financial institutions or other regulated institutions which require the monitoring of financial transactions.[33]

The FAFT describes the risks of VCs as follows. Virtual currencies are attractive to criminals and terrorist not only because they are not regulated generally, but also because they entail 'excessive secrecy' and are transnational in scope.[34] The absence of governmental regulation is compounded by the problem of asymmetry of information between the administrators of VCs and users, as well as between administrators and governmental authorities. The problem of 'excessive secrecy' is said to arise because of 'user anonymity' and 'anonymising services'.[35] User anonymity arises because the user's virtual world identity cannot be traced back to their real world identity. For example, in a bitcoin transaction the virtual (bitcoin) addresses of the sender and receiver are recorded in a public ledger, but this does not result in the identification of any specific bitcoin, or the identification of any specific user.[36] Anonymising services are 'tools and facilities which

---

32 South Africa Reserve Bank, *Position Paper on Virtual Currencies*, Paper number 02/2014, National Payment Systems Department, 12 March 2014, 7.

33 Ibid.

34 FATF, *New Payment Products and Services (NPPS) Guidance*, FATF, Paris, 2013.

35 He, above n 4, 27.

36 Kristin Finklea, *Dark Web*, Congressional Research Service, 7 July 2015, 11 <https://fas.org/sgp/crs/misc/R44101.pdf>.

are created for the specific purpose of obscuring the transaction chain, so that the source of a VC transaction cannot be traced.[37] Both the identity of the user of the VC and the internet transactions of that user are hidden through tools, such as darknets and mixers. The best known example of a darknet is Tor, which is an 'underground distributed computer network' that conceals the IP internet address of a customer/user.[38]

Different VC schemes have different risk profiles. There is a lower risk in a decentralised VC scheme of 'rent seeking' by persons at the centre or of a financial collapse.[39] At the same time decentralised VC systems pose higher Anti-Money Laundering/Counter-Terrorist Financing (AML/CTF) risk than centralised VC systems in that they have a greater opportunity for anonymity.[40] Under a decentralised VC system, such as bitcoin, transactions involving value transfers are identifiable by bitcoin addresses which are not linked to any specific individual in the real world; and there is no central supervisory body which makes it difficult to detect suspicious transactions.[41]

The FATF has issued a guidance note for countries in applying the AML/CTF Recommendations to VCs. The guidance, which was originally issued in 2014, has been updated in 2015, so as to assist countries to understand the evolving risks of VCs.[42] A VC which is traded on the Internet will usually involve 'no face-to-face customer contact', may permit 'third party funding from anonymous sources'[43], and may allow 'anonymous transfers, if the sender and recipient are not adequately identified'.[44] Applying a risk-based approach to VCs, the FATF considers that a convertible/open VC scheme is higher risk than a non-convertible/closed VC scheme because it allows illicit monies to move 'into an out of fiat currencies (legal tender) and the regulated financial system'. For this reason the

37 He, above n 4, 6.
38 Finklea, above n 36, 12.
39 Ibid.
40 FATF, above n 7, 9.
41 FATF, above n 22, 11.
42 Ibid.
43 Ibid 15–16
44 FATF, above n 7, 5–6, 8; and FATF, above n 22, 6.

FATF considers that greater attention should be given to 'VC nodes – i.e. points of intersection that provide gateways to the regulated system'.[45] This would mean greater regulation of convertible VC exchanges which should be required to carry out Customer Due Diligence (CDD) when exchanging VC for fiat currencies, [46] report suspicious matters where they arise, and provide ongoing monitoring of higher risk customers.

Liberty Reserve Case Study[47]

The Liberty Reserve case study provides a useful practical example of how a VC scheme can be so abused that the scheme must be prohibited, and not just regulated. On 28 May 2013 the US Attorney announced that a grand jury indictment had been issued against six executives of a Costa Rican virtual currency and money transmitter company, Liberty Reserve.[48] The indictment alleged that Liberty Reserve was one of the 'principal means by which cyber-criminals around the world distribute, store and launder the proceeds of their illegal activity'.[49] The US prosecutor accused Liberty Reserve of being the VC scheme of choice for organised criminals, who committed a variety of crimes, including 'credit card fraud, identity theft, investment fraud, computer hacking, child pornography, and narcotics trafficking'.[50] The indictment went further by alleging that nearly 'all of Liberty Reserve's business derived from suspected criminal activity',[51] a staggering allegation, given that it processed 55 million transactions involving 'more than $6 billion in criminal proceeds over a six and half year period.[52] The Liberty Reserve case was presented as the largest money

---

45 FATF, above n 22, 6.

46 Ibid 12.

47 See David Chaikin, 'The rise of virtual currencies, tax evasion and money laundering' (2013) 20(4) *Journal of Financial Crime*.

48 Santora, Marc, William Rashbaum and Nicole Perlroth, 'Online Currency Exchange Accused of Laundering $6 Billion', *New York Times*, 28 May 2013 <http://www.nytimes.com/2013/05/29/nyregion/liberty-reserve-operators-accused-of-money-laundering.html?_r=0>.

49 *United States of America v Liberty Reserve SA et al*, Indictment, Redacted 13 Cr. 368 (S.D.N.Y. 2013) United States District Court, Southern District of New York.

50 Ibid [9].

51 Ibid [10].

52 Ibid [10].

laundering case in history, with 45 bank accounts used throughout the world, including accounts at one of Australia's leading banks.

Despite the technological sophistication of Liberty Reserve, the modus operandi of the alleged money laundering was nothing new. Users of Liberty Reserve were able to open up an account at Liberty Reserve without any verification of their identity, and then conduct business between themselves, using Liberty Reserve's VC (called LRs) for payment. Users were prohibited from making direct transfers of real currency into their accounts; instead, users were required to make deposits through 'third-party exchanges' located in countries with weak financial regulation, such as Malaysia, Russia, Nigeria and Egypt.[53] Third party exchangers were allowed to buy LRs in bulk and distribute LRs by sale and purchase to LR users. This provided a high level of user anonymity which was further enhanced through multiple layering techniques, resulting in no 'centralized financial paper trail'.[54] Liberty Reserve also pretending to comply with Costa Rica's AML law, and when it could no longer fake its AML compliance, it went underground, attempting to transfer millions of dollars to a dozen shell company accounts in Australia, China, Cyprus, Hong Kong, Morocco and Spain.[55]

The law enforcement operation against Liberty Reserve involved co-operation with agencies in 13 countries. US criminal prosecutions were successful against the founder of Liberty Reserve, Arthur Budovsky, who was sentenced to 20 years imprisonment based on a plea of guilty to conspiracy to commit money laundering,[56] while his fellow co-defendants pled guilty to various charges, including operating an 'unlicensed money transmitting business'.[57] The Department of Justice closed down Liberty Reserve by seizing the company's websites and domain names, obtaining bank account freezing orders in a number of countries, and issuing the first

53 Ibid [18].
54 Liberty Reserve Press Conference Prepared Remarks of U.S. Attorney Preet Bharara, 28 May, 2013.
55 *United States of America v Liberty Reserve SA* et al, above n 49, [29].
56 Department of Justice, 'Founder of Liberty Reserve Pleads Guilty to Laundering More Than $250 Million through His Digital Currency Business', *Press Release*, 29 January 2016.
57 *United States of America v Liberty Reserve SA et al*, above n 49, [24–8], concerning Liberty Reserve's difficulty in obtaining a money transmitting license in Costa Rica.

section 311 order under the Patriot Act, which excluded Liberty Reserve (and its promoters, users and facilitators) from access to the US financial system.[58] The effect of this law enforcement operation was to ensure that Liberty Reserve and any potential business offshoot were destroyed. [59]

The Liberty Reserve case shocked the VC community into enacting new and improved AML compliance. This was not the first case against a VC business; for example, E-Gold and its founder were successfully prosecuted in 2008 for operating an illegal money-transmitter business, as well as money laundering relating to the trafficking of stolen credit and debit card numbers.[60] The significance of Liberty Reserve was its scale and its tremendous growth within a short period of time. While US prosecutors were ultimately successful in the Liberty Reserve case, there were difficulties in mounting a complex VC case which involved time consuming and expensive law enforcement resources. The US government was aware for some time of the principals of Liberty Reserve; the principals had set up their operations in Costa Rica precisely because they had previously been convicted of running an illegal money transmitter business in the United States.

AML Strategies and Reform

The Liberty Reserve Case raised questions as to the scope of AML regulation of VCs and whether additional measures are required to deal with online money laundering and/or virtual money laundering. The main focus has been on improving the private sector's role in the prevention of money laundering. This raises an important issue. How can the AML system, which was first developed to deal with real-world financial institutions, be adapted to the virtual environment? The FATF has produced 4 landmark reports on payment methods (1996), internet payment systems (2008), new

---

58 See Department of Justice, *US v Liberty Reserve SA et al*, Indictment & Supporting Documents, <https://www.justice.gov/usao-sdny/pr/indictment-supporting-documents-us-v-liberty-reserve-et-al>.

59 See Lawrence Trautman,' *Virtual Currencies Bitcoin &What Now After Liberty Reserve, Silk Road, and Mt. Gox?'* (2014) 20 Richmond Journal of Law and Technology 13 < http://jolt.richmond.edu/v20i4/article13.pdf>.

60 See Kim Zetter, 'Liberty Reserve Founder Indicted on $6 Billion Money-Laundering Charges', *Wired*, 28 May 2013 <https://www.wired.com/2013/05/liberty-reserve-indicted/>.

payment methods (2012) and prepaid cards, mobile payments and internet-based payments (2013), which have a direct bearing on issues pertaining to VCs, as well as 2 reports on VCs, covering definitions and risks (2014) and risk-based guidance (2015). However, countries have been slow in applying the FATF guidance, and in creating comprehensive AML regulation of VCs and participants in the virtual world.

The Liberty Reserve case highlighted the necessity for law enforcement and businesses to understand how new payment products and services pose new money laundering and terrorist financing risks. Care must be taken that any new regulation does not inhibit innovation in businesses and technology, such as new payment systems and delivery mechanisms. Any reform of regulation of VCs should adhere to a number of principles, including competitive neutrality, so that AML/CTF regulation applies 'equal treatment to all providers of similar products or services'.[61] The Australian Government in its 2016 review of the Anti-Money Laundering and Counter-Terrorist Financing Act 2006 (AML/CTF Act) accepted the importance of competitive neutrality' in the design of any reform.[62]

The Australian Government review identified various deficiencies in the law, and recommended a number of changes so that convertible VCs would be subject to comprehensive AML regulation.[63] A significant weakness has been the definition of 'e-currency' in section 5 of the AML/CTF Act,[64] which does not capture VCs that are supported by an algorithm, rather than backed by a physical item. In addition to recommending expanding the definition of 'e-currency' to include crypto-currencies, such as bitcoin,[65] the review suggested that the AML/CTF Act regulate the activities carried out by VC exchange providers, for example the provision of ATM services for VCs.[66]

61 Australian Government, *Report on the Statutory Review of the Anti-Money Laundering and Counter-Terrorism Financing Act 2006 and Associated Rules and Regulations, Attorney-General's Department*, Commonwealth of Australia, Canberra, April 2006, 43.

62 Ibid 5, 190.

63 Ibid 14–19.

64 E-currency is defined as an 'internet-based, electronic means of exchange…backed either directly or indirectly by precious metal, bullion … and not issued by or under the authority of a government body…'

65 Australian Government, above n 61, 45.

66 Ibid 49.

Another important recommendation of the Australian Government review was to expand the AML/CTF Act to cover digital wallets (virtual currency wallets, VCWs), and digital wallet providers.[67] VCWs have been defined as a 'means (software application or other mechanism/medium) for holding, storing and transferring bitcoins or other virtual currency'.[68] The justification for extending AML laws to VCWs is that they are functionally similar to bank accounts held by customers with a commercial bank. VCWs can be used for purchasing goods and services online or offline, as well as transferring value to and receiving value from third parties. VCWs are also similar to bank accounts in that there is no upper limit in the value which can be deposited in the virtual account. Another feature of VCWs is that they will store a user's personal and financial information in a digital format, which makes them vulnerable to theft. That security is a major challenge for crypto-currencies is demonstrated by the numerous thefts of bitcoins by hackers who steal the private keys of owners which are stored on computers.[69]

Conclusions

Although VCs have not been subject to regulation by monetary authorities, they are increasingly fulfilling some of the functions of national currencies. The classification of VCs based on their relationship to the real world is important for regulators, especially anti-money laundering policymakers. Crypto currencies, such as bitcoin, which are mined through use of algorithms, convertible to real world currencies, and are not subject to central administrative oversight, pose the greatest risk of money laundering. The Financial Action Task Force has issued a number of guidelines in relation to the risks of VCs, and jurisdictions, such as Australia, are responding by increasing the regulation of VCs. The challenge for any new regulatory scheme is to ensure that the benefits underlying the bitcoin technology – blockchain – are secured while the misuse of the technology are curtailed.

---

67 Ibid 44–5. The review suggests that the precedent of section 9 of the *Payments Systems (Regulation) Act 1988* could be used.

68 FATF, above n 7, 7.

69 Extance, above n 19.

Chapter 8

The Future of Digital Currency

David Chaikin, Ronald Tucker and Arun Kendall

David: This is an open Questions and Answers (Q&A) session whereby members of the audience may ask the Panel questions, and the panel may engage in a discussion of this topic.

The Australian Digital Currency and Commerce Association

David: In August 2015 the Australian Senate Economics References Committee produced a report entitled *Digital Currency Game Changer or Bit Player* (Senate Report).[1] The Australian Digital Currency and Commerce Association (ADCCA) made a significant submission to that Report. Ronald Tucker is the chairperson of ADCCA. Could you firstly, Ronald, explain what is the ADCCA?

Ronald: ADCCA was established about 18 months ago to help represent the interests of the emerging digital currency industry. This is a new tech industry is based on the 'block chain innovation'. There are about a dozen digital currency companies that specialise in bitcoin as well as block chain development solutions. ADCCA is the voice of the industry at both the national and international levels. It brings together stakeholders and encourages connections 'between merchants, industry, governments, reg-

---

1 Australian Senate Economic References Committee, *Digital Currency Game Changer or Bit Player*.

ulators, financial institutions and influential policy forums'.[2] ADCC facilitates discussions about the technology, its risks and the opportunities. We consider that if the industry is to progress it must work with stakeholders, particularly incumbents. We have worked closely with the Senate Economics References Committee to raise important questions during the open Senate hearings over the last 9 months. The Senate Report recommended that Australia embrace the new technology, that a graduated approach (to regulation) be adopted, and that this be 'light touch'. In our view, this is the type of framework which is needed for an emerging technology.

Bitcoin – Governmental Approaches

David: There are different governmental positions in various countries concerning bitcoin. What are the factors that influence some countries to ban bitcoin, for example, China, while others adopt a light touch regulatory approach?

Ronald: The key is probably education and awareness around what the technology is and what it can mean for their economies. With new technology there will often be a reaction, with some countries more front footed and other countries more reserved. The international trends show that important jurisdictions are embracing the technology. The UK Chancellor of the Exchequer has declared that if London is to remain as the world's leading financial centre, it must embrace the underlying financial technology (FinTech) of digital currencies, and ensure that the right regulator settings are put in place.[3] The UK Treasury's report of March 2015 recommended much of what is found in the Senate's Report, especially concerning a light touch approach and graduated requirements for new entrants

---

2 Australian Digital Currency and Commerce Association's website <http://adcca.org.au/>.
3 James Quinn, George Osborne embraces bitcoin as London aims to be centre of global financial technology revolution, *Telegraph* (UK), 6 August 2014 <http://www.telegraph.co.uk/finance/currency/11014508/George-Osborne-embraces-Bitcoin-as-London-aims-to-be-centre-of-global-financial-technology-revolution.html>.

into the market.[4] Similarly a Senate Committee report in Canada[5] echoed a number of the recommendations in the Australian Senate Report. In the United States, bitcoin has been declared a commodity,[6] while the EU has also viewed bitcoin as having some of the features of a currency.

Is Bitcoin a Currency?

David: And from the regulatory perspective, is bitcoin a currency? Does it have the characteristics of a currency from an economic perspective? Is it a medium of exchange, store of value, or a measure to price goods? Does it have any of those characteristics today or will it in the future?

Arun: For some people, digital currency may be a store of value, but it is intangible in one sense. Government issued currency has a linkage to a concept of physical currency. There is an irony here in that a lot of transactions that take place in the payments space are digital in nature without actual cash being used, so there is question whether even digital currency is virtual.[7]

Ronald: How is the new innovation of digital currency working now? It is being utilised in three major ways. Firstly, bitcoin, which is just one expression of the block chain technology, is being used as a currency. It is

---

4 UK HM Treasury, *Digital currencies: response to the call for information*, March 2015 <https://www.gov.uk/government/publications>. (See p. 3: 'The government considers that while there are clear barriers to digital currencies achieving widespread use in their current form, the 'distributed ledger' technology that underpins digital currencies has significant future promise as an innovation in payments technology.'); (See p. 9: '[There is a] good case for proportionate regulation at this time, to provide a supportive environment for legitimate digital currency users and businesses').

5 Report of the Standing Senate Committee on Banking, Trade and Commerce, Digital Currency You Can't Flip this Coin, June 2015 <www.senate-senat.ca/banc.asp>. (See p. 8 'light regulatory touch – almost a hands off approach.)

6 Luke Kawa, 'Bitcoin Is Officially a Commodity, According to U.S. Regulator', *Bloomberg*, 18 September 2015 <http://www.bloomberg.com/news/articles/2015-09-17/bitcoin-is-officially-a-commodity-according-to-u-s-regulator>.

7 'More than 89% of Australian currency is already digital – it exists and is transferred only in electronic dematerialised form between accounts with authorised deposit-taking institutions'. See APCA, Submission to the Senate Economics References Committee's Enquiry into Digital Currency, 8 December 2014 <http://www.apca.com.au/docs/2014-submissions/submission-on-inquiry-into-digital-currency.pdf>.

also being used as commodity. Further, it is a payment processing network, thereby crossing three main pillars in a way which hasn't been achieved before. This is due to the cryptography and the mathematical security underlying the technology. There have been a number of papers written over the past 40 years suggesting that digital currencies are potentially a global currency or commodity, but it is only in today's environment that this potential may be realised.

David: But what is bitcoin doing that current payments objects or mechanisms are not doing? Is it doing something better? What service is it offering, in terms of the interests of consumers or businesses? What is it about bitcoin and digital currency that make them attractive? Is it just going to remain something which is on the sidelines? I know people in the industry would love for digital currency to expand because it is good for business. But why should we think that it is going to become anything bigger?

Ronald: It is the world's first real chance for a truly global currency to exist, if it is adopted, which is a strong possibility, given that it has reached a critical mass of awareness in such a short time. It is often one of the most difficult things for any product or service to become accepted and adopted. Even though most people do not use bitcoin or digital currencies right now, 85% of people are at least aware of it, and somewhat familiar with it. Digital currencies are still not the most user friendly; it's still very much in the early days of email, when you would have to enter your own TCPIP settings and dial into the university server, and go through the hassle that you would have had to about 25 years ago to utilise email. Eventually we had the Hotmails of the world and the AOLs come along, and it was only then that emails became a lot more user friendly and accessible. Bitcoin is still in those early days. There is a lot of competition in the market place of digital currency. I expect that there will be an arms race on in the next two to five years, resulting in a greater acceptance of digital currency and the emergency of the world's first global currency.

Arun: I think that's a very important question there David, because in a sense any kind of disruptive technology needs to fill a gap, essentially that is not being satisfied by the market. The use of bitcoin is potentially a disruptive technology, but we should remember that is only one of a number of digital currencies.

Ronald: There are over 700 digital currencies in play today.

Arun: Exactly, there is actually quite a lot of scope for digital currencies in terms of overseas transactions, because the current banking system doesn't do well or doesn't do overseas transactions cheaply. We have many examples in the remittances sector.

Ronald: Cost is an important consideration. Digital currencies (DCs) involve a fraction of the cost of traditional payments systems because DCs are driven by a peer-to-peer network, much like in the early days where we had NAPSTER, and we know what effect that that had on the music and eventually on the film industries.[8] This is why DCs will affect the banking sector and the established financial services sector, particularly in remittances and moving money across borders.

The Risks in Digital Currencies

Arun: Is there a risk in digital currencies? It's interesting that you mention NAPSTER which was a brand name for innovation, but where is NAPSTER today?[9]

Ronald: Exactly.

---

8 David Z Morris, 'Bitcoin is not just digital currency. It's Napster for finance', *Forbes*, January 21, 2014 <http://fortune.com/2014/01/21/bitcoin-is-not-just-digital-currency-its-napster-for-finance/>.
9 At one stage NAPSTER, the 'Internet killer app' for sharing music files, had 80 million registered users, NAPSTER was eventually shut down after a US court issued injunctions for breach of copyright, and media companies such as AOL, Yahoo and Microsoft, embraced the music sharing software. See Brad King, 'The Day the Napster Died', *Wired*, 15 May 2002 <http://www.wired.com/2002/05/the-day-the-napster-died/>.

Arun: Is there any analogy there with bitcoin at all?

Ronald: Digital disruption is what we are talking about and NAPSTER is one of the earliest and most meaningful innovators. The exact commercial path forward is not clear; we ultimately saw iTunes adopt and adapt (music sharing software) on a far bigger scale. We must keep an open mind about what will happen. We should ask a lot of questions around the regulatory settings and get that correct.

David: Protecting the integrity of one's own national currency is a key attribute of sovereignty, so is there a possibility if bitcoin became too successful, governments would feel threatened and would ban its use as a currency. One of the reasons why China may have banned banks from using bitcoin[10] is that it has not worked out how it is going to affect their exchange control regime and the internationalisation of their currency. So it is one thing to digitally disrupt taxi services, but if you digitally disrupt currency, you are operating in completely new territory. Up until now, the history of the innovators and marketeers of digital currencies hasn't been a good one. A lot of them have gone out of business, or the people who have been operating digital currencies have been gaoled for fraud or money laundering. So it's very difficult if you are a futurologist, trying to predict what's going to happen in this area, is it going to displace other currencies? That is based on the assumption that consumers will find it sufficiently attractive to use it and governments are going to stand by and not intervene.

Arun: That is a very interesting question, because a lot of the economic direction of Australia is set by the Reserve Bank of Australia, and that includes setting monetary policy. What bitcoin does is actually operate outside that sphere, so it is difficult to know what will happen in the future. A body like APCA is agnostic on this issue, because as we have submitted to the Senate,[11] presently there is not enough data to understand how and

10 There is also a concern about the misuse of bitcoin for money laundering purpose.
See Simon Rabinovitch, 'China bans banks from bitcoin transactions', *Financial Times of London*, 5 December 2013.
11 See APCA, Submission to the Senate Economics References Committee's Enquiry

the extent to which bitcoin is being used; it's only when it reaches a certain tipping point and there is more consolidation in bitcoin offerings that there will be enough trust for it to be used more widely, and not merely in small retail settings, such as in coffee shops.

Ronald: Exactly.

David: Although I did notice when I was searching the web that a law firm in Sydney advertises that it accepts bitcoin as payment.

Ronald: There is a couple of major game changers in this space, and incumbents are already considering adopting the (distributed ledger) technology to their own services. There will be some evolution, and better adoption. It is not common knowledge that in the US and now in Australia, PayPal through its subsidiary Braintree allows the adoption and payment of bitcoin, via Paypal.[12] If you have a merchant who takes PayPal, you can now pay in bitcoin. One of the world's largest digital currency companies, San Francisco-based Coinbase, is now in 35 countries, and they are growing as a real contender. Coinbase has just partnered with Visa, and they are offering a Visa card, so anywhere where Visa is accepted, you will be able to spend your bitcoin and use your bitcoin.[13]

Mining of Bitcoins

David: And can you explain how you mine bitcoin. How do you get it?

Ronald: Some very smart people –– computer scientists, cryptographers, and technologists –– have developed this technology. Essentially it is just

into Digital Currency, 8 December 2014 <http://www.apca.com.au/docs/2014-submissions/submission-on-inquiry-into-digital-currency.pdf>.

12 Alex Hern, 'Paypal to accept bitcoin through subsidiary Braintree', *Guardian*, 11 September 2014 <http://www.theguardian.com/technology/2014/sep/11/paypal-bitcoin-braintree-overstock-reddit>.

13 Cade Metz, 'Coinbase Just Debuted the First Bitcoin Debit Card in the US', *Wired*, 20 November 2015 <http://www.wired.com/2015/11/coinbase-unveils-countrys-first-bitcoin-debit-card>.

the peer-to-peer network whereby computing power is dedicated to managing and administering financial transactions. If you lend your computer power you can be rewarded in bitcoin. Today, you need some serious computing equipment to mine bitcoin, not merely your home computer. I remember one of the more successful bitcoin miners in Australia started five years ago, with 500 computers; he was at school and during the summer break he wired all the computers together and started mining and he did quite well. The second way is to purchase bitcoins from one of the digital currency companies; there are about nine companies in Australia, where you can purchase your bitcoin online.

Arun: I understand that here is no physical ATM machine where you can exchange bitcoin for cash, or vice versa.

Ronald: That's correct. However, in Canberra you can buy bitcoin at the ATM in the Canberra Centre and use it to buy coffee and a bus pass.[14]

David: But it's not a physical, it's not like a currency? There's nothing physical.

Ronald: That is correct.

David: It's information; it's data isn't it?

Ronald: Exactly.

Bitcoin Compared to Currencies

David: And I understand there's a limit on how much bitcoin can be mined. Can you explain what that is and why it is the case?

---

14 Matthew Raggatt, 'Canberra's Canberra latest addition to bitcoin boom with high-tech ATM', *Sydney Morning Herald*, 19 July 2014 <http://www.smh.com.au/digital-life/digital-life-news/canberra-latest-addition-to-bitcoin-boom-with-hightech-atm-20140719-zuri2.html#ixzz3u9WWNSOP>.

Ronald: We really are striking at the heart of what is money? And money is a ledger; it's a system of account, that's what it stands for, and rather than doing it with paper dollars in our wallet, it is simply recorded online, on the web and we call it the block chain ledger or the bitcoin ledger. There are websites you can visit and actually see every transaction on the bitcoin ledger that is moving from a to z. So it's different and unique. It's anonymous as cash, but it's very much an auditor's dream in that there is a ledger of account that is recorded and you can see the transactions all movements. To answer your question there will be 21 million bitcoins ever in existence, we have mined about half of them, and there are 14 million floating around. They're mined at a steady, stable and predictable rate, it's part of a mathematical formula that underpins it and for every bitcoin that's created, essentially the next one becomes twice as hard to create and solve, the last bitcoin will be mined in 2140.

Arun: What happens then?

Ronald: Well that's just it. There is a finite supply. Its intrinsic value in a monetary sense relies on the fact that it is a limited supply. Once bitcoin has been mined, what's the incentive for continuing to use it? Well the transactions still need to move, people are still paying for goods and services in bitcoin, so the miners will continue to be incentivised for providing the computing power to move, the transactions and they can still be rewarded for that.

Arun: This conversation itself explains why bitcoin is such a challenge and will be so difficult to get the trust of people.

Ronald: To fully answer these questions, it would take another day or two of panel sessions and you would need economists, bankers and computer scientists and maybe philosophers. I would recommend a very useful website –– http://bitcoinproperly.org –– which is a six-minute video explaining exactly how the technology works and what it can mean for the future.

Arun: How you see my organisation APCA as being a sort of model, for the future for your organisation?

Ronald: I think it's we're big proponents of this of ADCCA, I mean digital disruption is here but it is important in many regards to make it perhaps a little less disruptive if we are able to, and I've always said that a city without stop signs and street lights and roundabouts is chaos, so it is important, and what we did with ADCCA, when coming to terms with what this technology means and the impact it is going to have on all key stakeholders, we look to an organisation to find out if something similar had been faced before. And there was, many years ago, not to the scale or extent, but as I understand it, and please correct me if I'm wrong, but you know about 25 years ago, there was a gentleman walked into one of the major law firms here with an idea to send funds electronically between banks and merchants and consumers, and it came to be known eventually as EFTPOS, at the time some participants thought it might be a little disruptive and scary and others saw an opportunity in it and as I understand it, an association was formed to help bring stakeholders together and address what the issues are and then properly regulate it and capitalise on it and this was a self-regulatory model, and we think it is one that makes a lot of sense for this industry as well too, being that there is no central authority around it and really the main vehicle to drive this are going to be businesses operating in this space, providing bitcoin, selling bitcoin, mining bitcoin. We modelled, we took a look at Aitkins and it makes a lot of sense on how we should shape up an engagement with government and with consumers and to get a good framework in place early on.

Role of Self-Regulation

Arun: What is your view of the role of self-regulation?

Ronald: We have several committees in the ADCC and the most important one right now is the anti-money laundering and financial crime committee. As I said before the block chain is an auditors dream, you can see every transaction from A to Z; it is still certainly preferable to know who the actors are behind it, who are the people using the technology and it comes down to making sure we have checks and balances as to the on ramps and the off ramps. We are creating a certification that's available to our members that have some rigorous built in stringent know your customer and AML requirements, so that in order for these companies to obtain the seal of approval, they will have to take their customers through ID verification properly and know who they are dealing with.

David: Any other questions?

Future Impact of Digitisation

Audience: If it's possible to digitise the majority of transactions which banks are involved in, what will be the impact on the financial world and the existing financial institutions, especially in Australia where we have a fairly protected environment for banks.

Ronald: It does, but it's a well organised one, which means if we reach out and communicate the advantages and benefits to applying these types of standards now, based on a pre-existing model, it would benefit the group as a whole, and it's perhaps more important especially as we move into a global digital economy that Australia does act as a group of stakeholders together and position us as a leader, certainly regionally, but there is a real opportunity to do it globally, that I think is actually going to be perhaps more difficult for a lot of other jurisdictions because it is in such a well-knit, tied off. So there is a few ways we need to do that, obviously the Senate's Economics References Committee Final Report put a set of recommendations through, as I understand it there is certainly some interest particularly from I don't want to say the new government but new leadership to adopt some of these recommendations with some expediency, we were expecting within the next 6 to 12 months so that's a help there, but even just sort of on a bit of a more granular level too when we talk about the relationships, I was fortunate enough to be a part of an informational luncheon about two weeks ago, and we did have some senior directors, and chairmen from some of the large organisations there, we had CBA and a number of the other banks, and it's about just having a real sort of garage talk, if you will, and go there is, it's going to be to everyone's benefit if we work together and communicate properly and see ourselves as one group, one collative, and it was well received, so I think we are making progress.

Contributors

Louie Bai

Louie Bai graduated with First Class Honours in the Discipline of Business Law at the University of Sydney Business School, with a thesis entitled 'Supervision of Online Based E-Finance.' Louie holds a Bachelor of Business with Distinction from University of Technology Sydney (UTS). Louie's research interests focus on the development of e-finance in China, including financial and quasi-financial services and e-commerce platforms.

David Chaikin

Dr David Chaikin is a Barrister and Chair of Business Law at University of Sydney Business School. His research interests include reform of trust laws, international financial crime, and shadow banking in China. He has previously held the position of Senior Assistant Secretary/Head of the International Criminal Law Enforcement and Security Branch in the Australian Attorney-General's Department, and Senior Legal Officer of the London-based diplomatic body, the Commonwealth Secretariat. David is the co-author of Corruption and Money Laundering: A Symbiotic Relationship. He holds a Doctorate in Law (Cambridge), a Masters of Law (Yale), and double degrees in Law and Commerce (UNSW).

Hui (Steven) Feng

Dr Hui (Steven) Feng is a research fellow at the Griffith Business School, Griffith University. Dr Feng's research interests are international political economy and post-communist transitions, with a focus on Chinese politics and political economy. His articles appear in major international journals such as *Political Studies* and *Review of International Political Economy*, and is a co-winner of the British Political Science Association's Harrison Prize 2014 for best paper published in *Political Studies*. Dr Feng is also a contributory editor of the journal of *Central Banking* (UK).

Eva Huang

Eva Huang is a lecturer in Business Law at the University of Sydney Business School. She researches and teaches in the areas of taxation and commercial law, focusing on comparative studies between China and developed countries, and is the founding and current editor of the Journal of Chinese Tax and Policy, the first English language journal with an exclusive focus on taxation policies and laws in China. She is also an Adjunct Associate Professor of the Department of Public Economics of Xiamen University, and an Adjunct Researcher of the Center for International Tax Law and Comparative Taxation of Xiamen University.

Arun Kendall

Arun Kendall is a lawyer working in the Industry Policy Department of the Australian Payments Clearing Association. During this time he has worked on a number of cross-industry policy issues including public consultation on the future of cheques in Australia, the development of the digital economy in payments, and the Australian Payments Plan for the Australian Payments Council. Prior to holding this position, he was Executive Officer for the Asia/Pacific Group on Money Laundering, an international body evaluating regional compliance with international anti-money laundering standards, and Manager of Regulatory Affairs for British Airways in the UK.

Antony Ting

Antony Ting is an internationally recognised scholar on the taxation of corporate groups and international tax avoidance by multinational enterprises. He publishes regularly in leading domestic and international taxation law journals, including the *British Tax Review, Canadian Tax Journal* and *Australian Tax Forum*. Antony's research on the taxation of corporate groups under consolidation is published as a monograph by the Cambridge University Press, UK. Antony is also a regular commentator on taxation issues in the media, both in Australia and overseas.

Ronald Tucker

Ronald Tucker is Managing Director at Bit Trade Labs and Chair at the Australian Digital Currency & Commerce Association (ADCCA). He has over fifteen year's professional experience in business development and hands-on commercial entrepreneurship with projects including: digital currency; government relations; marketing (traditional and digital); publishing; SME retail/wholesale; and experiential marketing, events & conferences.

Anthony Wong

Anthony Wong is the principal of a multidisciplinary law and consulting firm, AGW Lawyers & Consultants, specialising in IT, IP cloud computing, Big Data, privacy and data protection. He is formerly chair of the New South Wales Government ICT Advisory Panel, member of the New South Wales Government Accelerating Digital Government Taskforce and served on the IT Industry Innovation Council for the Australian Department of Industry for 3 years. He currently serves as a board member of the International Federation for Information Processing (IFIP), an umbrella organization working in the field of information processing headquartered in Austria, established in 1960 under the auspices of UNESCO.

Zhaozhao Wu

Zhaozhao Wu is a lawyer with Teddington Legal, and a postgraduate research student at the University of Sydney Business School. Her research interest includes the legal risks of online marketplaces and digital platforms in China, and has published papers in China's legal and tax policies, and phishing attacks in e-commerce. She holds a Juris Doctor from the University of Sydney, a Bachelor of Laws from China University of Political Science and Law, and a Master of Management majoring in Accounting from the University of Melbourne. She is admitted as a lawyer in the Supreme Court of New South Wales.

Mary Wyburn

Mary Wyburn is a senior lecturer in Business Law at the University of Sydney Business School. Before joining the Business School Mary worked as a solicitor with Baker & McKenzie and as a legal officer with the Australian Copyright Council. She has acted as a consultant to copyright industry organisations. Her current research focuses on the ownership of intellectual property rights in commercialised research.

Printed in Australia
AUHW010920250220
324216AU00003B/36